Attract, Then Repel:

Why Are Candidates' Abandoning Your Employment Process?

by

Dr. Karen Hills Pruden, SPHR

dp Rochelle

PO Box 9523
Hampton, Virginia 23670
1(757) 825-0030
infodprochelle@aol.com

First published by dpRochelle 10/1/16

Edited by: Dr. Karen Hills Pruden

ISBN: 978-0-9862389-8-7

Printed in the United States of America, Hampton, Virginia

ACKNOWLEDEGMENTS

To the strong women who raised me: my mother, Beverly; my grandmother, Pearl; and my Aunt Nancy.

Special Thanks to:

Dr. Cynthia Davies

Dr. Libi Shen

Dr. Christina Anastasia

This book is based in whole or part on the doctoral dissertation of Karen Hills Pruden entitled: The Recruitment Process and Applicants' Decision to Complete the Employment Process: A Phenomenological Study.

Preface

After working in human resources for almost two decades, I remain curious as to why candidates withdraw from the employment recruitment process. Many times these candidates are more than qualified for the position to which they apply. Organizations spend thousands of dollars annually to attract qualified candidates only to lose them before given a chance to make an employment offer.

The Bureau of Labor Statistics (2012) estimates that over the 2012-2022 decade there will be 50.6 million job openings to be filled. There will not be enough qualified candidates to fill vacant positions over the next 10 years, according to this projection. Employers will need to attract, retain candidate interest, and hire to meet staffing needs. This book documents the results of a study that examined why candidates withdrew from the employment recruitment process. It should be used as instructional material to help employers audit the organization's employment recruitment process to improve candidate retention rates. The implications of the findings are that those factors that adversely affect the experiences and perceptions of employment candidates are under the control of the employer.

Table of Contents

List Of Tables

List Of Figures

Chapter 1

Introduction

"The transition from higher education to professional employment is a major life change for many college seniors" (Hurst & Good, 2009, p. 570). These seniors are no longer looking for pocket change or gas money; some are looking to jump-start their professional career by finding employment in their educational field of interest. Others are looking to employ the concepts and theories they were exposed to in their education. Some students may approach the search for professional employment in a nonstrategic manner with the goal to attain employment. The recent college graduate begins by submitting resumes and/or accepting interview requests, with the goal in mind to initiate the employment process to obtain the desired position (Boswell, et al., 2011). Not all candidates choose to complete the recruitment process with prospective employers. Some candidates make the decision to disengage or withdraw from the employment recruitment process. This qualitative phenomenological study was a method of inquiry to understand the lived experiences and perceptions of candidates who have voluntarily disengaged or withdrew from one recruitment employment process and who have accepted an employment offer from another organization.

Background of the Problem

The Bureau of Labor Statistics (BLS) projects that positions that require postsecondary education will grow faster than those that require a high school diploma or less (BLS, 2013). The BLS projects that this will result from the need to replace workers who retire or leave the workforce permanently (BLS, 2013). Nineteen of the thirty occupations projected to grow fastest from 2012 to 2022 will require postsecondary education for entry (BLS, 2013). Over the 2012-2022 decade, 50.6 million job openings are expected, 67.2 percent of these positions are projected to come from replacement needs (BLS, 2013). Employment candidates will be seeking employment to fill these vacant positions.

In April 2013, Talent Q conducted a survey of 526 college graduates and undergraduates, asking them about their experiences of applying for jobs. The results of the study were that four flaws in the employment recruitment process frustrated participants. These areas were lack of communication, duration of selection process, behavior of interviewers, and finding out that the position was different from what was advertised ("Through the eyes" *Talent Q*, 2013).

The employment recruitment process and information learned about the organization help form the applicant's perception of the company and can be important factors in the decision to continue or withdraw from the process. Information, which may be considered, is

2

training opportunities, advancement opportunities, human resource policies, compensation, and corporate reputation (Dineen & Williamson, 2012). These attributes shape the assessment of the potential employer by the applicant.

An individual's expectation in their ability to be successful in a position is determined by the job's requirements, and how the applicant measures personal attributes up against those requirements (Bosak & Sczesny, 2008). Walter, et. al (2012) found that often candidates form beliefs about a position before applying for a position. The desired attraction is mutual between applicant and employer resulting in the subsequent job offer where the employer selects the applicant (Suptan, 2011). Recruitment is not only about attracting candidates. Organizations must maintain the interest of these candidates throughout the process to the point of acceptance of the job offer (Martin, et. al, 2010).

Statement of the Problem

There is limited research exploring the perceptions of candidates who are attracted to organizations, begin the employment recruitment process, but choose to discontinue the employment process. Organizations are losing qualified candidates due to factors within the employment recruitment process (Dineen & Williamson, 2012). The general problem is there will not be enough qualified candidates to fill vacant positions over the next 10 years, as projected by the

Bureau of Labor and Statistics (Employment Projections, 2013). It is in the best interest of employers to create positive candidate experiences during the recruitment process to maximize the number of candidates. The specific problem is that each step in an organization's employment recruitment process must facilitate that each job applicant has a positive candidate experience (Ployhart, 2006).

The organizational desirability thematic has increased in significance during employment searches (Gomes & Neves, 2010). "Over the last several years, recruitment researchers have acknowledged that initial attraction to a firm is necessary for applicants to be motivated to process company-related information and apply for openings" (Slaughter & Greguras, 2009, p. 16). The desired outcome is an attraction of mutual preference where both the applicant and employer identify shared values resulting in job offer acceptance (Suptan, 2011).

With budgets, shrinking, organizational leaders must realize that recruitment is more than just money, benefits, and perquisites, which make an organization an attractive employer (Nolan & Harold, 2010). Employers are competing for candidates from the same qualified population. Although recruitment budgets differ among organizations, the desired result is the same, which is to hire qualified candidates; thereby, completing the employment recruitment process (Ployhart, 2006). Organizations need candidates

4

who make the decision to continue in the employment recruitment process to the point of job offer.

Purpose of the Study

The purpose of this qualitative phenomenological study was to explore the lived experiences and perceptions of candidates who voluntarily disengaged or withdrew from one recruitment employment process and who accepted an employment offer from another organization. Participants in the study were candidates seeking an entry-level professional position. Participants in this study had no history of working in any professional occupation. Participants voluntarily withdrew from at least one organization's employment recruitment process. Participants also, had accepted an employment offer from another organization. These two requirements allowed the participants to share lived experiences and perceptions when accepting a job offer and when participants voluntarily disengaged during the recruitment process.

Significance of the Study

This research topic is significant because there is an ongoing need for qualified employees within organizations. Baby Boomers (born 1946-1964) are exiting the workforce in record numbers (Hurst & Good, 2009). Organizations will need to hire qualified employees who can immediately contribute to the organization. Personnel requirements vary based on organizational demographics. However, all organizations hire personnel at some point. Organizations must first attract candidates prior to the applicant completing the application process. This study sought to understand through the lived experiences and perceptions of candidates who voluntarily disengaged or withdrew from the employment recruitment process.

The aim of this research was to provide organizational leaders with information by exploring the phenomenon participants experienced during recruitment processes, and its relationship to the continuation in the employment process. This phenomenon was pursued in depth through the lived experiences and perceptions of candidates who withdrew or disengaged from an employment recruitment process within 12 months of participating in the study. Participants also have accepted an employment offer from another organization. These two requirements allowed the participants to share lived experiences and perceptions when accepting a job offer and when participants voluntarily disengaged during the recruitment process.

The result of this study was to provide information to organizational leaders about how candidates perceive the recruitment process and how such perceptions affect the recruitment and hiring process. The results of the study were unique to this specific sample. However, the study can be replicated among candidates who meet the participation criteria in other areas.

Significance of the study to leadership.

Organizational representatives have several opportunities to strengthen the interest of candidates in the employment process. The first exposure is through recruitment activities such as job fairs or employment office personnel (Saks & Uggerslev, 2010). Another opportunity is the employment application or any online application program used by the organization to collect applicant information (Chapman & Webster, 2003). The interview stage is another opportunity where organizations may strengthen the interest of a candidate (Huffcutt, Van Iddekinge, & Roth, 2011), whether the interview is over the telephone or in person; each interaction influences the candidate. This research sought to understand through the lived experiences and perceptions of candidates who voluntarily disengaged or withdrew during the recruitment employment process. Participants also accepted an employment offer from another organization. These two requirements allowed the participants to share their lived experiences and perceptions when accepting a job offer and when voluntarily disengaging during the recruitment process. The results of this study will provide organizational leaders and recruiters with an understanding as to why the organization may not be receiving the desired return on invest for recruitment dollars.

The job search process is self-regulated (Boswell, Zimmerman, & Swider, 2011) and can be altered at the will of the job seeker.

Previous research described career selection as lucid, goal-focused conduct (Kulkarni & Nithyanand, 2013). Little is known about the factors that affect the desirability perceptions of candidates (Cable & Graham, 2000). This study is significant to leadership because leaders and organizations must be aware of those elements of recruitment, which influence the decision making of an applicant. Certain factors are within the control of the organization such as: use of online tools to promote the employment brand (Alwi, 2009); use of training managers to assess talent (Davidson, 2000); use of personality and skill assessment testing, incorporation of employment brand into the organizational brand (Trueman, 2012); use of applicant tracking software (Smith & Rupp, 2004); ensuring applicant follow-up throughout the recruitment process (Ma & Allen, 2009); and utilizing staffing firms when recruiting is specialized. Other factors, that affect the recruitment process such as conversations with peers, friends, and family members, are more difficult to change.

The decision of the applicant to apply for employment is critical in the recruitment process. The objective of the employer is to get the applicant to seek employment with the organization and to complete the entire employment recruitment process. Recent research shows there is a link among job choice decisions and social influence and social comparisons (Kulkarni & Nithyanand, 2013). The opinions of friends also influence candidates' job choice decisions (Kulkarni & Nithyanand, 2013).

8

College and employer partnerships are a great source of recruitment. "Younger workers, who plan to enter the workforce in the next 5 to 10 years, are a critical population for employers" (Martin, et al., 2010, p. 167). Leaders must recruit and hire these younger workers to replace the existing Baby Boomers in the work force (Fort, et al., 2011). College graduates are an available qualified candidate pool for these vacated positions (Martin, et al., 2010).

Employers want to hire qualified employees who can immediately contribute to the organization (Martin, et al., 2010). These employees must be a fit for the organization, where they can merge into the culture with little difficulty (Hurst & Good, 2009). To fill vacate positions with these candidates; organizations must first attract these candidates This study is significant to leadership because it can be duplicated to aid leaders in understanding those elements of the recruitment process, which affect the decision of an applicant to complete the employment process.

Nature of the Study

The selection of the research method and design was considered against the nature of the problem to be studied and the type of data that was required. Data was analyzed to explore, classify, and interpret the lived experiences and perceptions of each participant. This data was self-reported, and analyzed to identify any reoccurring themes and meanings. Because the data was collected through the use of interviews from participants, describing in their own words their lived experiences and perceptions, the appropriate design was phenomenological.

A qualitative study identifies individuals as, "active, mindful, aware of what is going on and able to make choices" (Al-Hamadan, 2010, p. 51). Emphasis is placed in part on the interpretation of the observations in research studies. This research sought to understand the lived experiences and perceptions of candidates who voluntarily disengaged or withdrew during the recruitment employment process. Participants have also accepted an employment offer from another organization. These two requirements allowed the participants to share their lived experiences and perceptions when accepting a job offer and when voluntarily disengaging from the employment recruitment process of another organization. A qualitative method was most appropriate to pursue in depth the subjective experiences and perceptions of the participants.

The researcher focused on the decision-making of the applicant to continue or withdraw while being exposed to the recruitment process. The researcher sought to explore the complex interrelationship of the phenomenon of the recruitment process and applicant decision-making while seeking entry-level professional employment. The design was appropriate because the data sought was subjective based on each participant's perception and interpretation throughout the recruitment process.

Researchers use phenomenology to scrutinize how humans view their surroundings and their role within a particular topic (Converse, 2012). In this study, the phenomenon was the employment recruitment process. The objective of this study was to explore through the lived experiences and perceptions of candidates, and the underlying reasons that led to their decision to voluntarily disengage or withdraw during the employment recruitment process. Participants had accepted an employment offer from another organization.

Actions in the recruitment employment process and practices can affect an applicant's decision to continue (Boswell, et. al, 2011). A job search begins with an employment goal, and then subsequent conduct to carry about that objective (Boswell, et. al, 2011). An applicant must complete the recruitment process to attain employment.

The central question for this study was what are the perceptions and lived experiences of candidates about the underlying reasons that led to their decision to voluntarily disengage, withdraw or continue in the employment recruitment process? The sub-questions were designed to pursue in depth connections between the employment application process, the interview process, applicant and employer communication, and the applicant's decision to continue or withdraw from the recruitment process.

Research Questions

R1: How do candidates describe their experiences regarding the method of employment application during the employment recruitment process?

R2: What are the lived experiences of candidates regarding the interview process during the employment recruitment process?

R3: What lived experiences did candidates describe as influencing their decision to voluntarily withdraw from the employment recruitment process?

R4: What lived experiences influenced candidates' decision to follow through the entire employment recruitment process to job offer acceptance?

Theoretical Framework

This study considered the application of three theories. The first is the theory of reasoned action TRA (Fishbein & Ajzen, 1975). This philosophy was relevant to this study because the theory advocates that there are three elements of human behavior intents: (a) attitude towards a behavior, (b) social pressure to engage in certain behavior, and (c) personal and moral norms (Fishbein & Ajzen, 1975). The theory was relevant, as candidates determined whether to move along the recruitment process based on interactions with company representatives or processes. Applicant interpretations are described by what the applicant deems as acceptable behavior by potential employer representatives based on previous exposure to the same behavior, societal norms, personal morals, or the social pressure to accept or reject certain behavior. For this reason, this theory was relevant for this study.

The second theory considered was Maslow's theory of human needs (Armache, 2011). This theory has five levels in a tiered manner from lowest level needs to highest-level needs (Armache, 2011; Maslow, 1954). Maslow's hierarchy of needs are: (a) physiological needs (Maslow, 1943); (b) safety needs; (c) belongingness needs (Maslow, 1943); (d) esteem needs; and self-actualization needs being the highest level (Maslow, 1943).

Each one of Maslow's needs in the hierarchy relate to fulfilling the intrinsic or extrinsic needs of an applicant (Maslow, 1943). Intrinsic needs are internal desires to perform a task, which gives an applicant pleasure (Maslow, 1943). Extrinsic needs are factors external to the applicant; for example, compensation or human resource policies (Maslow, 1943). The applicant may employ elements of Maslow's theory when selecting a prospective employer based on the applicant's awareness that a particular need can be fulfilled. This theory supports the study because there is an assumption that there was a matching criterion when an applicant selected an organization to seek employment. An applicant is consciously or subconsciously attempting to satisfy an intrinsic or extrinsic need by the selection of that employer.

Job seekers' opinion of the people employed for a specific company affect the achievement of the staffing efforts of the organization (Walter et al., 2012). Candidates are attracted to organizations based on their similarities (Cable & Judge, 1997). An applicant who seeks to work for an organization with similar values uses the person-organization (P-O) fit theory (Kim et al., 2005). This is the comparability between the applicant and the potential employer (Kim et al., 2005). An applicant who supports clean water initiatives seeks out organizations that support water conservation and purification efforts. Walter, Wentsel, and Tomczak (2012) conducted a study of 97 marketing participants in regards to the impact of *P-O fit* in employer attraction. The results of the study were *P-O fit* had a

14

greater influence on employer attraction when applicant intentions for employment is in the distant future (Walter, Wentsel, & Tomczak 2012).

This philosophy was relevant to this study because the longer the time span between the job seeking of the applicant and the desired employment increased the impact of P-O fit in the selection of the organization for employment.

Theory of Reasoned Action (TRA).

This theory coined by Ajzen and Fishbein (1975) suggested employment seekers who are confronted with certain behavior will rely on their belief that this behavior will lead to a certain outcome. As a result, candidates evaluated the outcome of the behavior to determine whether to continue in the employment process. These job seekers lack first-hand knowledge of what the organization is like (Goldberg & Allen, 2008), and therefore, relied on their reasoning to determine further interaction with this potential employer. Judgment formed by the applicant about concerns of *fit* with the job or the organization influenced the applicants' continued participation in the employment process.

Theory of reasoned action is a subjective process (Fishbein & Ajzen, 1975). An organization's website, a recruiter's demeanor, or a television commercial can influence the decision of an applicant to continue with the employment process. Candidates take the information no matter how incomplete, and form an overall impression of an organization. TRA links organizational culture to recruitment activities by affecting what interactions candidates attend to; by affecting how behavior is interpreted from data or dealings; and how this behavior sways applicant response and decisions (Ma & Allen, 2009).

In recruiting materials, the desired impression is that this organization is where the candidate wants to work. Corporate websites are filled with information to aid the applicant in the employment decision-making process. Candidates make the decision to seek employment based on the interactions with company processes and representatives no matter how limited. The theory of reasoned action is used in this scenario.

Maslow's Theory of Human Needs.

Maslow's theory of human needs, pursue in depth what needs the applicant is trying to please during employment. If the organization has what the applicant is seeking, the applicant performs at a high level.

This information helps organizations to develop recruitment plans to attract these candidates. These needs are: (a) physiological; (b) safety; (c) belongingness; (d) esteem; and self-actualization (Maslow, 1943). Anthropological relations and communal needs of candidates are vital characteristics of recruitment (Maslow, 1943).

Organizations must consider what the organization has to offer the applicant. Organizations must know and understand Maslow's theory of human needs when seeking to understand the concerns of candidates during the recruitment, job choice, and the application process.

Person-Organization Fit Theory.

According to the person-organization (P-O) fit theory, candidates are attracted to organizations that have similar values as the candidate. "This theory is traced to Schneider's attraction-selection-attrition (ASA) framework" (Cable & Judge, 1997, p. 546). According to ASA, there is mutual attraction between an applicant and organization based on similarities between the two. Judge and Bretz (1992) found that there was a connection between the ethics of an applicant and the applicant's perceived ethics of the organization. Candidates who value water conservation, recycling, and other environmentally conscious processes seek to work for organizations that participate and support such green initiatives.

Candidates who place a high priority on quality time spent with small children seek out employers that have human resources benefits that allow the applicant to merge employment within the family structure with little disruption. Organizations often implement flexible workforce processes such as work schedule flexibility, telecommuting arrangements, on-site day care facilities, and flexible benefit plans to increase compatibility between the organization and

17

its workers (Cable & Judge, 1997; Kim et al., 2005). Candidates seeking to balance time between work and family time find scheduling flexibility benefits attractive.

Candidates, who place a high value on material possessions, associate a higher pay with the ability to acquire such possessions (Cable & Judge, 1997). For these candidates, salary is a major consideration in selecting what job or company to pursue. Compensation structures that recognize individual performance based pay is preferred over group-based pay. With individual performance as the trigger for recognition and recompense, the applicant maintains total control over pay and the ability to acquire a certain lifestyle. In a group-based pay structure, the applicant loses total control in exchange for partial contribution to performance. Consequently, the employee loses control over the results and outcomes of performance influencing compensation.

Coldwell et al. (2008) established that candidates are attracted to organizations displaying compatible ethical values. Applicant expectations for organizations who demonstrate ethically responsible behavior has risen over the years. Ethics are included in a corporation's social responsibility (CSR). CSR is an organization's obligation to conduct business that is good for society beyond what is required of the law (Coldwell et al., 2008). CSR is also a component of an organization's reputation, which is an attractor for employment candidates. Recent interest in P-O fit is sketched to the attraction-selection-attrition (ASA) framework (Cable & Parsons, 2001), that proposes candidates and organizations are similarly interested in each other established on comparable objectives and principles (Cable & Parsons 2001).

Definition of Terms

The following key terms were used to help clarify general concepts concerning this phenomenological study.

Candidate. An applicant who has been placed in the candidate pool for employment consideration (Bosak & Sczesny, 2008).

New entrants. Individuals who are new to the workforce (Boswell, Zimmerman, & Swider, 2011).

Organizational attractiveness. The readiness of an applicant to pursue jobs or accept employment offers in a business (Tsai & Yang, 2010).

Recruitment. "A sequential and multi-stage process that permits an organization to target prospective employees with specific skills" (Gomes & Neves, 2011, p. 697).

Recruitment Brand. A component of the organizational brand. Organizations create the recruitment brand using tools for work force planning for the selection and placement of qualified personnel (Rai & Kothari, 2008). Examples of tools of this brand are: (a) job descriptions, (b) qualifications required for positions, (c)

19

motivational attributes, (d) online human resources application programs, and (e) information about the organization (Rai & Kothari, 2008).

Recruitment Practices. An organizational specific cue strategy that directly communicates positive detailed information or provide job seekers with an avenue to acquire detailed information (Collins & Kanar, 2013).

Assumptions

Simon (2006) stated assumptions adhere to the spirit of prudence to be effective.

An inherent assumption pertaining to this study was that participants would be accessible and readily available to participate in the study. This study is based on the experiences of candidates. The candidates have withdrawn or disengaged from an employment recruitment process. Participants have also accepted at least one entry-level professional employment position. The assumption was that the participants were truthful in their responses in describing their lived experiences and perceptions in their professional job search process. Another assumption was that the candidates would be able to articulate the reason for withdrawing or continuing in the employment recruitment process. As a researcher, my personal assumption was that there would be enough participants who had disengaged from the employment recruitment process. A final assumption was that the candidates were prepared to interview for those positions that they provided feedback for during the semi-structured interviews for the study.

Scope

The scope of this study was the recruitment experience for entry-level professional employment among candidates. This study was conducted within a four to six-week period from March to May of year 2015. The researcher interviewed until saturation was reached. Semi-structured interviews were used to understand the lived experiences and perceptions of the participants and Nvivo10© software was used to interpret the results.

Limitations

Organizations differ based on characteristics of industry, number of employees, and size of the organization. It is difficult to precisely compare one organization to another based on varied components, and differences. Qualitative research is difficult to generalize because the data is local and particularistic (Christensen, Johnson, & Turner, 2011). Another challenge to the results of the study was the arbitrary manner in which the candidates could change their mind, based on unrelated factors in the study. These factors include medically related situations, applicant transportation issues, and family related situations. All participants completed the research interview.

The study was conducted with participants who spoke English only. This was a limitation of the study, by the researcher's choice to administer English speaking interviews. The job seeking experience of non-English speaking candidates may vary from that of English speaking candidates.

An examination of collected works found there was a deficiency of research regarding at what stage organizations attract candidates (Gomes & Neves, 2011). There was a possibility of researcher bias. The researcher works in the human resources field. By working in a position that is responsible for recruiting, the researcher's professional experiences and knowledge could have affected how the study was conducted. Finally, different researchers can interpret the same phenomenon differently.

The results of this study are only relevant to the lived experiences and perceptions of the selected participants for this study. Generalizability is where the results of a study can be attributed to a larger population (Neumann, 2006). The sample for this study were candidates who had withdrawn or disengaged from an employment recruitment process within 12 months of participating in the study and who has accepted a professional employment offer.

The outcome of this study can be attributed to this sample populace only. The demographics for the participants are in the control of the researcher and are deliberate to understand only the lived experiences and perceptions participants who are actively sought professional employment. Any deviation to requirements for participants could have altered the results of the study and influenced the outcome of such research. This study had three areas of confinement: (a) demographics (b) participants selected for the study and (c) the geographic location of the selected participants.

Delimitations

Qualitative research can pose a number of challenges for the researcher, specifically when dealing with emotions of interviewees (Mitchell, 2011). The researcher prepared for interviewees who became emotional when discussing employment related matters. Qualitative interviewing can cause participants to reveal distressing feelings. The researcher prepared to address emotional issues during the interview process and after the interview (Mitchell, 2011). A researcher's knowledge and experience can also sway the way a study develops (Griffiths, 1996). This is known as researcher's bias (Richens & Smith 2011).

The researcher for this study has more than two decades of experience in staffing and recruiting for organizations. The experience and knowledge of the researcher could have detracted from the data scrutiny used in this study. In addition to the effects of bias, the researcher could have also been affected by the emotional response of the participants. Strategies were put in place by the researcher to assist in reflecting and coping with the researcher's own emotions. One strategy that was employed by the researcher was to ask probing follow-up questions of participants' answers when needed to ensure answers documented were the views of the participants. During this process of probing and self-reflection the researcher could have augmented an understanding of the phenomena being researched (Mitchell, 2011).

Chapter 2

Review of the Literature

The purpose of this qualitative phenomenological study was to explore in depth the lived experiences and perceptions of candidates who voluntarily disengaged or withdrew from one recruitment employment. Participants must also, have accepted an employment offer from another organization. These two requirements allowed the participants to share their lived experiences and perceptions when accepting a job offer and when voluntarily disengaging during the recruitment process.

The perspective of the applicant, who has initiated the employment process through application, then withdrew, and subsequently accepted an employment offer from another organization has not been widely researched. During conversations with organizational representatives or exposure to company information, the candidate may discover that his/her objectives are not a fit with the organization's objectives. The candidate may choose to withdraw from further consideration in the employment process. With an organizational focus on recruitment, it is important for leaders to understand what factors in the process are influencing candidates from completing the process.

Socio-economic inclinations, including the advancement of employment forces and a progressively viable market, have caused leaders to focus on recruitment (Gomes & Neves, 2010). Economists predict large-scale baby boomers to retire from the work force in the next 5-10 years (Hurst & Good, 2009). These workers will take with them company knowledge and years of experience in the industry. This battle for 'knowledge

Workers have been dubbed the "war for talent" by the media (Collins & Kanar, 2013). These employees are hired to produce and analyze ideas needed to fill and maintain these positions with education and computer skills that are the foundations of organizational innovation (Collins & Stevens, 2002). Employers will recruit and hire qualified candidates, to fill the knowledge gap left by existing workers (Collins & Stevens, 2002).

Recruitment researchers have theorized that recruiting success is determined by job seekers' comprehension of recruitment information, accuracy of expectations, and candidates' motivation to pursue in depth what the organization has to offer (Walker, Berneth, Field, & Becton, 2012). Candidates can have a different perspective about a potential employer based on where the applicant is in the employment recruitment process (Walter, et al., 2012). Organizational leaders need to understand that employment recruitment processes and practices affect the ability of the applicant to sustain interest in the job and/or organization which may influence the candidates desire to complete the *employment process to job offer acceptance* (Walter, et al., 2012).

For today's labor force, money is not the sole motivation (Martin, et al., 2010). Other factors such as environment, autonomy, benefits, job-fit, training opportunities, and advancement potential may be equally as relevant to the applicant (Martin et al., 2010).

Organizations must clearly inform potential candidates of their stance on human resource policies, ethical policies, company values and its mission. These factors are part of the recruitment information that candidates consider when seeking employment. Previous research (Coldwell et al., 2008; Wayne & Casper, 2012; Yue, 2012) stated organizations strive to hire qualified personnel who can immediately contribute their talents to the organization. Informing the public of the organization's stance on policies, corporate values, and the mission, may increase the likelihood of drawing qualified candidates with the same qualities. Organizational attraction is the first step in the employment seeking process.

When candidates find such practices attractive, this increase the value of the organization within the candidates' mind. The value of an organization is determined not only by its lucrativeness and future growth projections but also by elements such as the revenue it produces for consumers through growth prospects to labor, the quality of employment opportunities it offers, its impact on the physical environment and brand and its contribution to the overall

27

quality of life (Trueman, 2012). Available employment opportunities influence the chance of the applicant to seek employment. Attracting qualified candidates to an organization, which does not have employment opportunities, affect the decision of an applicant to seek employment in the future. Such employment opportunities determine value, and value is an element of organizational attraction.

The job search process is an applicant self-regulated process. It is the conduct through which energy and time by the applicant is used to obtain evidence about the labor market to produce occupational opportunities (Boswell et al., 2011). There are three main types of intentions in the job search process: (a) intentions to apply for work; (b) intentions to pursue work; and (c) intentions to accept a work (Gomes & Neves 2011).

In each stage, the applicant must make the decision to complete the process. Candidates must identify an employment goal, commit to pursuing a goal, and activate job search behavior to acquire the goal (Boswell et al. 2011).

Historical Overview

Early recruitment focused on vocational behavior research literature and tested job or organization choice by anticipated job satisfaction (Rhynes, 1991). The focus was on the job and its compatibility to the applicant. Researchers' interest later moved to the organizational corporate image and how the applicant used this perception when determining to pursue employment (Gatewood, Gowan, & Lautenschlager, 1993).

In 1997, Judge and Cable's research results of 38 interviewers making hiring decisions for 93 candidates, focused on applicant personality, organizational culture, and organizational attraction (Cable & Judge, 1997). These factors were addressed in isolation of one another. The researchers found that the employer representative considered all three attributes in the overall assessment of the potential employee. The results suggest that an interviewer's assessments of a candidate have a large impact on that interviewer's recommendations of that candidate for hire which directly impacts the overall hiring results of the organization (Cable & Judge, 1997).

"Most recruitment research has investigated a single activity or stage of the recruitment process" (Saks & Uggerslev, 2010, p. 351); while this study seeks to understand a number of factors that involve human interaction that may influence an applicant. These factors are: (a) organization follow-up to application, (b) length of the selection process, (c) the interview, (d) and organization communication throughout the recruitment process.

There is interest in the role that human interactions play in the recruitment process. Candidates continue to inquire, apply for, pursue, and accept employment in that order. There may be additional screening practices depending on the organization;

however, the main steps remain. There is limited research to capture what influenced those candidates to abort further consideration for employment with an organization. This research attempts to understand what role employer recruitment processes and practices play in the decision of the applicant to continue or complete the process.

Recruiting became important when organizations began competing for qualified talent from the same pool of candidates. For this reason, it is pertinent that once qualified candidates are attracted to an organization, representatives maintain that relationship until they no longer are interested in the candidate. Organizations must seek to find a way to uncover what candidates are seeking in the recruitment process (Martin et al., 2010). These same organizations must identify how desired attributes are identified by the qualified applicant, and through what source.

Researchers have found that candidates are looking for job postings to list not only the job requirements, but also what the employer has to offer the candidate (Feldman, Bearden, & Hardesty, 2006). Using a 3-factor experimental design the previous researchers conducted two studies to examine the types of information provided by potential employers regarding the company, the job, and the work context (Feldman, Bearden, & Hardesty, 2006). The results of the study were that ads that included specific information were perceived by candidates as being truthful (Feldman, Bearden, & Hardesty,

30

2006).

Online websites can create a bridge or a roadblock to the interest of an employment applicant in an organization by its words, and images (Lyons & Marler, 2011). Organizations cannot afford to lose one applicant's interest. Recruiters must make prominent those attributes the candidates are seeking, so such attributes can be readily identified and considered by the potential applicant.

The recruiting success of a firm is impacted by internal attributes as well as external factors that are beyond the organization's control such as joblessness, and the obtainability of employment within the applicant's field (Bernardian, Richey, & Castro, 2011). Elements within the organization must be analyzed and considered in recruitment strategies. Internal factors such as employee behavior, timeliness of the duration of the employment process, and user-friendly online application programs are within the organization's control to adjust if required.

Meta-analytic proof shows that job and business features and individual concerns of supposed fit and employment expectations, (Bernardian et al., 2011) forecast applicant attraction. The staffing process, and material learned about the organization along with the perception of the applicant of the company can be important factors in the decision making process to select an employer. Such attributes considered may be training opportunities, advancement opportunities, human resource policies, compensation, and corporate reputation to shape the assessment of the applicant regarding the image of the firm. This analysis results in the perception of an applicant regarding organizational fit.

Recruiting is one way organizations increase the pool of employment candidates or target potential employees with specific needed skills (Rhynes, 1991). An organization's ability to attract qualified candidates while utilizing the least amount of financial resources would be the ideal recruiting strategy. Organizations are seeking to gather a pool of prospective qualified candidates for current and future staffing requirements (Gomes & Neves, 2010). Budgets and funding streams are shrinking among organizations. Leaders are looking to minimize expenses in every area including the area of recruitment.

Leaders should first look internally to understand the actions of employer representatives throughout the employment process that may be influencing candidate retention. Interactions with the receptionist, the hiring manager, or the new hire drug- testing site may adversely influence a candidate's decision to continue in the employment recruitment process (Martin, et al., 2010). Recruitment success varies depending on the targeted population. Ployhart (2006) found that the job search process differs across diverse groups. Given this discovery, employment representatives must identify and understand what each targeted group find attractive and adjust applicant interactions based on each individual applicant (Ployhart,

2006). The cookie-cutter approach of one-size-fits-all will not be successful with every applicant. Each applicant has different needs.

Current Findings

The process of recruitment is critical to the staffing practice of organizations, specifically when unemployment is low and there is high competition for skilled workers (Gomes & Neves, 2011). Younger workers entering the workforce are a pertinent population for companies that are predicting a loss of workers due to Baby Boomer retirements (Martin et al., 2010). Organizational recruiters should determine what this population of qualified candidates find attractive about the company, and what role the recruitment process played in the attraction.

An effective recruitment strategy is necessary to garner the initial attraction of those candidates who may be unfamiliar with the organization. This attraction is a necessary first step to motivate these individuals to complete the application process and apply for employment (Slaughter & Greguras, 2009). Organizational attraction and the desire to apply for a job in that organization are two different constructs predicted by different things (Aiman-Smith et al., 2001). The desire to pursue a job is achieved by an initial attraction followed by additional behavior to bring about that goal (Boswell, Zimmerman, & Swider, 2011). Attraction can be exclusive of intentions to pursue a job. Job pursuit encompasses additional behavior plus attraction (Slaughter & Greguras, 2009).

There is no *act* required past the initial appeal in the attraction phase. The interest from an individual can drop after the attraction with no further action. Continued attraction matures past the initial stage of attraction, moving the individual into the desire to pursue a job. In this case, the completion of application or the submission of a resume is used to predict an individual moving towards the applicant phase, demonstrating the desire to pursue a job.

The desire to pursue a job is determined by the actions of the prospective applicant. Pre-hire requirements of application, resumes, and interviewing, once completed by the applicant signifies a continued interest in obtaining employment with the organization. Information about an organization's training, salaries, career progression opportunities and job security policies can be credited to a candidates' affirmative valuation of an organization (Gomes & Neves, 2011) and such information can promote the prospective applicant's continued attraction to the organization. The desire to pursue a job is an attraction, plus job pursuit intention. An area of emphasis in the human resources recruitment process is the interaction between the applicant, organizational representatives and processes, and the role each element of the organization plays in influencing potential candidates to complete the employment process. Organizations need to find the answers to what factors drive the applicant to complete the employment process with the organization.

Approximately 1.5 million college graduates from all disciplines enter the job market annually (Wayne & Casper, 2012). Within the first year, 84% are employed full-time (Wayne & Casper, 2012). Employers must capture the interest and attention of this applicant pool as the job search process may be concurrent with the final year of college. The attractiveness of an organization to a graduate may extend beyond a year during the job search process. At times, participants accept job offers more than a year prior to their anticipated graduation date.

Potential applicant awareness can be conveyed through testimonies of others, marketing and advertisement on the internet and as well as through the interaction of the applicant as a customer with a potential employer. Candidates also become aware of organizations through interaction with company representatives in the college career center. The way these job seekers process recruitment information influences how effective recruitment activities are in persuading job seekers to seek employment with the organization (Walker et al., 2012). Understanding the reasons important to the intent of the applicant to apply is pertinent for effective staff planning and goal setting (Gomes & Neves, 2011).

Recruitment activities have evolved using the internet (Trueman, 2012). Research on recruitment has evolved as well (Walker, Berneth, Field, & Becton, 2012). In 2003, Chapman and Webster administered a web-based survey to human resources managers in 125 organizations. The results were that employers were increasingly using more information technologies on the internet in Human Resource (HR) practices such as applicant screening and selection (Chapman & Webster, 2003). Even with the ease of technology, there are candidates who choose not to follow-through with the employment recruitment process. This research attempted to uncover why these candidates withdraw through the lived experiences and perceptions of participating candidates.

In 2006, Cable and Kang found that there was limited research on how organizations manage their online images during the recruitment process. Goldberg and Allen's (2008) research of 806 randomly assigned college participants to 73 various websites revealed 70% of companies were using a form of online staffing practices. Lyons and Marler's (2011) research investigated which corporate online attributes correlated organizational attraction that resulted in applicant self-selection behaviors. The next year, scholars suggested organizations could monitor and revise organizational diversity sensitivities through the design of staffing information on the organization's website (Walker et al., 2012). Organizations are losing qualified candidates prior to employment offer (Aiman-Smith, Bauer, & Cable, 2001). With the increased use of online technologies in hiring practices, the use of these technologies must also be reviewed to determine its role in impacting candidates desire to proceed in the employment recruitment process.

36

A gap in literature exists regarding an applicant's motivation to continue and complete the recruitment process with an employer (Walker et al., 2012). This research study was a method of inquiry to understand the lived experiences and perceptions of participants who voluntarily disengaged or withdrew during the recruitment employment process. Participants must also, have accepted an employment offer from another organization. These two requirements allowed the participants to share their lived experiences and perceptions when accepting a job offer and when voluntarily disengaging during the recruitment process.

Recruitment

Organizational recruitment activities are largely based on the needs of the organization. The potential employer is looking for qualified candidates whose skills and education match certain criteria (Kulkarni & Nithyanand, 2013). The goal of the employer may be different from the desires and needs of the potential candidate. If this is the case, representatives of the organization should be aware of these differences and how these differences influence recruitment goals (Kulkarni & Nithyanand, 2013).

This study can assist recruiters with information to understand at what stage in the recruitment process the applicant is influenced to abort or continue the employment process. The results of the study provide organizational leaders and recruiters with actual candidate feedback about what areas in the employment process require adjustment to be in line with the recruitment goal. This study was a method of inquiry to understand the lived experiences and perceptions of participants who voluntarily disengaged or withdrew during the recruitment employment. Participants must also, have accepted an employment offer from another organization. These two requirements allowed the participant to share their lived experiences and perceptions when accepting a job offer and when voluntarily disengaging during the recruitment process.

Recruitment is a multi-stage process, ultimately aiming to target and attract prospective employees (Gomes & Neves, 2011). In the area of recruitment, cross- cultural knowledge is vital as demands for talent poses escalating challenges to effectively attracting desirable candidates (Ma & Allen, 2009). Most recruitment literature is published in English, which may prevent non-English speaking qualified candidates from applying for employment. As diversification intensifies, dissimilar human capital has become a critical element for a firm's success (Ma & Allen, 2009). Increasing demand for diverse talent forces firms and institutions to recruit key employees of all cultures and races (Ma & Allen, 2009). Recruitment functions, as a critical tool of persuasive communication, plays an important role in attracting the right diverse talent (Ma & Allen, 2009); however, very little is known about the effectiveness of recruitment practices across cultures (Ma & Allen).

This study has no global perspective. Previous research reveal candidates look for diversity cues in corporate information when assessing potential employers (Aiman- Smith et al., 2001; Coldwell et al., 2008; Walter et al., 2012). For this reason, organizations must consider how diverse candidates perceive the recruitment message and what organizational elements speak to these candidates.

Five dimensions influenced job seeker reactions and decisions across the three phases of recruitment (Ma & Allen, 2009). In the generating candidates phase, organizations are most interested in attracting qualified candidates to the organization and its opportunities (Ma & Allen, 2009). In the maintaining candidates phase, organizations are concerned about maintaining candidates' interest while simultaneously evaluating candidates for job and organizational suitability (Ma & Allen, 2009). In the influencing job choice phase, organizations selected the candidates believed to fit best, and hope that most of these candidates are equally positively disposed to the organization (Ma & Allen, 2009).

A key mechanism linking candidates to the impact of recruitment activities on outcomes is theory of reasoned action. According to the theory of reasoned action (Fishbein & Ajzen, 1975), job seekers facing incomplete information will use whatever information they have as signals regarding the job and organizational characteristics (Ma & Allen, 2009). This theory is relevant for this study because an applicant can disengage at one of the three stages in the employment recruitment process.

The applicant's employment recruitment perspective can differ from that of the potential employer. In the generating applicant's phase, the applicant is seeking compatibility with the job and/or organization (Ma & Allen, 2009). In the maintaining candidates' phase, the applicant is concerned about the accuracy of the advertised information for the position compared to the verbal description of the job as expressed by company representatives (Ma & Allen, 2009). In the influencing job choice phase, both the organization and applicant may seek the same desired identification, job-fit (Nolan & Harold, 2010).

Job fairs and direct contact with college placement offices are ways companies are able to recruit and hire the best and the brightest participants before they graduate. For some participants, the college placement office is the initial introduction to organizational representatives. Both parties are invested in the acquaintance. Participants are seeking information about organizations and available employment opportunities. These organizations rely on the knowledge of the participants regarding the company to motivate the applicant to seek out the organization for employment. The ultimate goal of the organizations is to hire qualified candidates who can immediately contribute to the organization.

Corporate Communications

Organizations rely on corporate website information to inform the public of its vision, mission, and values, which are incorporated in their human resource practices and policies. Organizations expand the recruitment audience using online websites. In 2008, Goldberg and Allen (Goldberg & Allen, 2008) found that over 70% of organizations at the time were using some form of internet-based recruitment. There are several advantages to using technology based recruitment software. Organizations are able to expand applicant pools with the use of internet-based software by removing any constraints caused by geographical locations of businesses. For convenience, interested individuals can apply for employment from any device with an internet connection. The internet is a work milieu, a tool for communication, information, and business (Lehmann & Konstam, 2011). It serves the dual role of providing company information while serving as a work environment by assisting the applicant through the application process. The internet can be used by organizations to provide desired company information to prospective candidates at minimal costs minimizing the potential recruitment costs.

In some cases, the use of the internet minimizes the costs associated with hiring employees. The Saratoga Institute includes six basic fundamentals to determine cost per hire: 1) marketing; (2) agency and search firm fees;(3) referral bonuses paid to workers; (4) travel costs incurred by both the organization's representatives and candidates; (5) relocation costs; and (6) company recruiter costs (including salary and benefits prorated if the recruiter performs duties other than staffing) (Davidson, 2000). These six factors account for 90% of the cost to hire (Davidson, 2000). Saratoga Institute adds an additional 10% to cover miscellaneous expense items such as testing, reference checking, bonding, employing unit staff time, administrative support and other minor expenditures (Davidson 2000).

Customers and Candidates

Organizational attraction is similar between customers and candidates. However, an applicant is seeking a long-term relationship with the organization that may not exist between the customer-organization interactions. A customer-organization interaction can be completed with one transaction. Whereas; the interaction of an applicant who becomes an employee can span a number of years. The same characteristics potential customers use to discern from which company to purchase a product or service can be used to discern which employer to apply for employment. The goals are different in terms of the length and scope of the relationship desired.

Every company representative throughout the employment recruitment process can serve as a brand actor of the organization. As the applicant move from one stage to the next, the role of the employer representative is to continue to market the organizational brand to assist the candidate in the decision-making that the job and/or organization is a fit for the applicant (Vallaster & Lindgreen, 2011). Just as employees promote the brand of the organization to customers, employer representatives serve the same purpose to employment candidates (Davies & Chun, 2012). Every element of the employment recruitment process has multiple messages for the applicant to aid in the determination to continue or withdraw from the employment recruitment process (Hemphill & Kulik, 2011)

Job Choice

The job choice process begins with an individual's evaluation of information obtained from recruiting sources. Although it is well known that the image of an organization affects the initial decisions of potential candidates, it is still unknown how candidates' beliefs affect their decisions (Bermudez-Edo et al., 2010). Kulkarni and Nithyanand (2013) conducted a study based on in-depth interviews of MBA students to look into the role of social comparisons and social influence of job choice decisions. While this study consisted of students of various disciplines not solely participants completing a MBA curriculum. The findings of these interviews are noteworthy. In this study, the researcher pursued in depth the lived experiences and perceptions of a variety of candidates to answer the four research questions revolving around applicant decision-making and the employment recruitment process.

Peers are viewed as more trustworthy than organizations (Kulkarni &Nithyanand, 2013) according to the interviews of MBA participants. The participants for this study sought entry-level professional positions. Social influence appears to be a key factor in job choice decisions for entry-level professional job seekers. Martin et al. (2010) used the Job Decision Factors Survey in a study of 400 undergraduates at a large university to capture the measure and influence of seven factors on job decisions. These factors were: (a) work environment, (b) autonomy, (c) compensation, (d) benefits, (e) advancement potential, (f) job fit, (g) and training opportunities (Martin et al., 2010).

The study targeted the recruitment and retention of candidates. The study indicated that these young workers were not willing to pursue certain entry-level jobs even when they offer competitive salaries. Research revealed simply money is not an attraction for these workers (Coldwell, et al., 2008). These workers require a less formal environment and they tend to favor flexible work attire policies in an informal loose communal structure (Martin et al., 2010). In order for an organization to attract these participants, these organizations must tailor benefit packages to fit the applicant.

Job Search

Job search, from a potential employee perspective, consists of three components: identify employment goals, (b) commit to pursuing goals, and (c) activate job search behavior (Boswell et al., 2011). There are three labels given to individuals seeking a job. An individual can be new to the workforce. Researchers label these job seekers as new entrants (Boswell et al., 2011). There is also a population of job seekers who were previously employed and who are no longer employed; researchers label this category of job seekers

44

as job losers and or unemployed (Boswell et al., 2011). The third category of job seekers are those individuals who are employed, however, they are seeking a new employer (Boswell et al., 2011). This study focused on individuals new to the professional workforce, known as new entrants (NE).

The 30 occupations with largest projected growth from 2012 to 2022 will account for 7.4 million new jobs, almost half of the projected employment growth (Bureau of Labor Statistics, 2013). These workers are categorized as new entrants (Boswell, Zimmerman, & Swider, 2011). This category includes college graduates, apprentices in skilled labor roles, enlistees in the armed forces, individuals who have returned for postgraduate study following a period of employment, and individuals with disabilities completing special education programs (Boswell et al., 2011). The participants for this study were new entrants (NE) to the professional job search market.

Online Employment Websites

Most firms have a corporate website, and it usually offers a broad range of information, such as the mission statement, strategic objectives, functional details, customers' profiles, history, and financial information, among other features. Globalization, the lack of geographical proximity, and the invisibility of many firms to media often imply the absence of previous interaction between potential candidates and the firm (Bermudez-Edo et al., 2010). This

45

underscores a maximum level of importance for the website of the firm.

Employers rely on their organization's website as a tool for recruiting employees (Goldberg & Allen, 2008). Over 70% of organizations are using some form of internet- based recruitment (Goldberg & Allen, 2008). The internet and various online information tools play a key role in conveniently placing organizational brands within the reach of interested candidates. There are two functions of the online presence: (a) building a brand image and (b) obtaining a direct response from users (Trueman, 2012). Company websites add to the organizational brand value online (Trueman 2012).

The virtual world influences applicant perceptions in the virtual world cultivating an active, online relationship between the company and the applicant to allow brand interpretations to ensue (Trueman, 2012). Information shared about available positions, qualifications for positions, compensation, benefits, and the organization are valuable for the applicant to utilize to make the decision of whether to seek employment.

Organizations can revive a diminishing reputation by coupling a positive brand, produced through activity online (Trueman, 2012). Those candidates who have limited knowledge of an organization benefit from the source of online information. A cybernetic environment can be a facilitator for transformation to build the corporate brand (Trueman, 2012). Information shared about available positions, qualifications for such positions, compensation, benefits, and the organization as a whole, are valuable information for the applicant to utilize to make the decision of whether to seek employment.

Researchers argued the brand, confidence, and status communicated via company websites could strengthen and positively influence perceptions about the organization (Alwi, 2009; Trueman, 2012). Organizations control the messaging placed on the corporate website (Alwi, 2009). There is limited control of inaccurate information placed beyond the company website, instantly for millions to read and see on other areas of the internet (Chapman & Webster, 2003). The result of such misinformation influences an applicant's decision to continue in the recruitment process (Trueman, 2012). There are existing influences of television, radio, and print media as well (Trueman, 2012).

Corporate websites are beneficial to the organization because these sites expose the corporate brand to potential candidates outside of the local geographical area (Bermudez-Edo, Hurtado-Torres, & Aragon-Correa, 2010). The internet provides a source for examination of occupation information, job openings, and company related information (Lehmann & Konstam, 2011). Organizational leaders can customize the information on the company website to appeal to a desired audience. Imagery and website wording can be

47

tailored to inform the various applicant groups needed for staffing needed positions

On a recruitment website, human resource policies such as flex scheduling and telecommute opportunities can be listed as well as spousal benefits and onsite daycare facility material. Research shows that online visual topographies and occupational information are related to organizational brand appeal (Lyons & Marler, 2011). Organizational leaders can positively influence brand image by proactively managing organizational diversity perceptions through the design of the recruitment website (Walker et al., 2012). A diverse workforce may provide the organization a needed competitive edge over industry competitors.

In the virtual world, a carefully designed website can express uniqueness and nurture confidence while encouraging an emotional connection between customers and the company (Trueman, 2012). The consequences of an online involvement by customers will result in positive or negative value judgments about company trustworthiness and brand value (Trueman, 2012). Users of corporate websites cultivate faith with regard to three characteristics of the company: ability, integrity, and benevolence (Bermudez-Edo et al., 2010). Trust infers the willingness to be vulnerable, grounded upon affirmative outlooks of another's behavior with consideration of risk and interdependence (Bermudez-Edo, et al., 2010). Ability means the potential to provide a quality result within the allotted time; integrity proposes that the company will honor promises as agreed upon; and benevolence means an organization considers the applicant's needs while striving to attain profits (Bermudez-Edo et al., 2010).

Lyons and Marler (2011) showed a website's visual features and occupational information are positively associated with organizational attraction. Visual features represent the overall aesthetic or state-of-the-art features of a website, such as complementary colors, images, vibrancy, and liveliness that keeps the user engaged (Lyons & Marler, 2011). A website should contain easy to get to employment information about the organization, existing employment opportunities, developmental opportunities and information on organizational values for potential candidates. Drawing on theory of reasoned action, an organizational website's visual features and employment content information should be representational of broader organizational perceptions such as organizational image (Lyons & Marler, 2011). Organizational image is characterized as an overall impression that is based on facts, beliefs, and feelings about an organization (Lyons & Marler, 2011). The most achievable strategy to advance organizational brand is to provide more information about the organization, which can be effectively portrayed on an organization's website (Lyons & Marler, 2011).

Organizational Attraction

Some participants may find their initial exposure to an

organization is when the company approaches the participant through some form of recruitment activity. Little is known about the reasons that influence an employment applicant, and to what degree this influence plays a part, in which organizations the applicant pursues for a job that may result in a job offer acceptance. Some candidates remove themselves from employment consideration prior to the job offer to the dismay of the organizational representatives. Organizations lose qualified candidates during various stages of the employment process after the initial applicant attraction. This is in direct contrast to the goal of recruiting qualified candidates to fill available openings.

Organizational attractiveness is the general desirability of a potential work relationship with an organization (Gomes & Neves, 2011). Attractiveness is important for recruitment purposes (Gomes & Neves, 2011). Organizations must know their targeted candidates' knowledge and beliefs about the organization before recruitment to identify the types of recruitment interventions that will provide the greatest return on investment (Slaughter & Greguras, 2009). Organizational attributes have become important in attraction (Gomes & Neves, 2011). These are the perception of what the organization provides regarding organizational policies and work conditions (Gomes & Neves, 2011). Candidates are influenced by these perceptions (Slaughter & Greguras, 2009).

50

There are two attributes suggested by researchers, which help formulate the opinion of candidates and the attraction to an employer. Organizational personality is the perception, which explores the beliefs found to influence initial attractions to organizations (Slaughter & Greguras, 2009). Recruitment equity is the value of job seekers' employer knowledge, which positively influences effectiveness of recruitment because of job seekers previous knowledge about the organization (Slaughter & Greguras, 2009). Aiman-Smith et al. (2001) in a study examined the relevance of four important factors: (a) pay, (b) promotion, (c) lay-off policy, and ecological rating. The study found job security and ecological factors were extremely important to job candidates (Aiman-Smith et al., 2001). Ecological factors of whether the organization supported sound *green* environmental practices mattered to at least some respondents. The study also found a potential recruit is very similar to a potential investor, especially in a robust market, in that the potential recruit will have a number of choices where to employ their human capital (Aiman-Smith et al., 2001).

Bermudez-Edo et al., (2010) conducted a study of 218 potential employees by utilizing a *dummy* online company and assessing the likeliness of participants to apply for the organization based on the online website. Researchers found candidates' experience bias due to a lack of trust in firms offering positions online, particularly when the firms are small, operate in a risky industry, or are relatively unknown (Bermudez-Edo et al., 2010). The study tested the theory of reasoned action (TRA) which views a person's intention to perform a behavior as the immediate determinant of the action to apply for employment. TRA is an extension of the theory of planned behavior; both theories explain the intention of an applicant to apply for a position influences subsequent behaviors to accomplish that task (Kulkarni & Nithyanand, 2013). The behavior of a person is a function of one's belief (Gomes & Neves, 2010). Those candidates who intend to find employment will proceed with the steps necessary to obtain employment according to the TRA theory.

Candidates are surrounded with imagery found on billboards, television, online, and cell phones (Robinson, 2004). Perceptions are also obtained through the respected opinions of others. Through the exposure to these resources, candidates determine whether the information is favorable or undesirable. Information deemed favorable might prompt the applicant to seek more information about the organization. The discovery of additional favorable information contributes to the applicant in making the determination to apply for employment. Continued favorable interaction with an organization's recruitment personnel, through the applicant's movement through employment processes, and the interview process may prompt the applicant to accept employment with the organization. In contrast, an encounter with undesirable information in any stage of the process from initial exposure to media, throughout the employment process, from application to interview, can cause the applicant to seek information and employment elsewhere.

Applicant Decision-Making

In the job search process, candidates must understand those factors that affect decision-making, and retain this information for as long as necessary to use, deciding one way or another regarding the selection of that company for employment (Brown, 2011). The first step in decision-making requires the problem to be identified and the desired outcome indicated (Hicks, 1999; Kartha, 2012; Watson, 2013). The problem must be analyzed realistically and honestly. In this study, the problem is that candidates are voluntarily disengaging and/or withdrawing from the employment recruitment process prior to the job offer. The desired outcome is for the applicant to accept an offer of employment with the organization. The focus of this study was the employment recruitment process, practices, and its influence on the candidate to continue in the process

Prior to moving towards the job search process, candidates determine what attributes of a prospective employer are desirable to them. In this examination, the applicant defines a set of criteria rated in order of importance. The list should identify the 'must have' attributes for an employer, as well as those attributes that would be 'desirable' to have, but may not exclude the employer from consideration. The researcher sought to understand the participants' lived experiences and perceptions and how the participants approached the examination stage in the decision-making process of moving through the employment process.

The second step in the decision making process is to develop alternatives (Anaya, 2013; Kartha, 2012). These alternatives are whether the participants search for employment through industry organizations, conduct an internet search for employment, or through attendance at job fairs. The researcher sought to understand the numerous means in which participants searched for employment such as: (a) answering employment ads, (b) networking with peers, (c) temp-to-hire opportunities, (d) job fairs, and (e) cold calling potential employers. Each of these methods, and any other methods expressed by the participant, helped the researcher understand the recruitment process involved, and what factors of the process affected the participant's decision to seek employment through the source chosen. At this stage, the participant considers any personal interests (Hicks, 1999) such as flexible scheduling, human resource policies, or telecommuting options as identified in Maslow's Theory of Human Needs (Maslow, 1943).

The next step in the decision making process is evaluation of alternatives (Watson, 2013). At this stage, the participant reviews all of the alternatives, and weighs the positive and negative aspects of each. In this stage, the participant examines information about potential employers. This information gathering can be obtained through: (a) answering employment ads, (b) review of employment information on the employer's website, (c) discussions with employer representatives, (d) networking with peers, (e) temp-to-hire opportunities, (f) job fairs, and (g) cold calling potential employers.

The participant (Watson, 2013) can study a detailed evaluation of each of the offerings of the organization with separate consideration for desired and required factors. Participants consider the work environment of the organization (Fort et al., 2011). This includes the physical and social context of work. Participants look for autonomy in scheduling and the opportunity to work independently (Martin et al., 2010). Compensation is evaluated in this stage (Fort et al., 2011). Employee benefits and potential for advancement are also weighed (Coldwell, Meurs, & Marsh, 2008).

Once the participant reviewed the advantages and disadvantages of seeking employment with each organization, the participant moves to make a decision (Kartha, 2012). The decision can take two forms. The participant decides to complete the employment process with an organization or the participant decides to forgo continued interest in seeking employment with an organization. During this stage, the researcher sought to understand those factors in the employment process that played a part in the participant's choice to seek employment with an organization and equally as important; the researcher sought to understand any adverse perceptions the recruitment process had on the participant's decision to forgo the application process.

Once the decision is made to forgo the employment process with an organization, no action is required of the participant. When the participant decides to seek employment with an organization, the participant follows the employer's application process and practices. Successful completion of the application process can move the participant to the status of 'applicant'. Kartha (2012) identifies this step as implementing the solution (decision).

The final stage of the decision-making is follow-up. Kartha (2012) states this step is where the applicant monitors the solution (decision). In this stage, job candidates complete any additional required steps to obtain employment such as interviews, pre-employment screenings, and the final act of whether to accept an employment offer. Completion of this stage denotes that the applicant has moved through the recruitment process of the organization to the point of accepting an employment offer.

"Organizations often connect organizational attraction with job pursuit decisions" (Aiman-Smith et al., 2001, p. 236). Studies have shown that some element has directed the interest of the applicant to the organization to inquire about employment (Lievens, Hoye, & Schreurs, 2005; Slaughter & Greguras, 2009; Walker et al., 2012). Recruitment research has confirmed candidates' attraction early in the recruitment process to be robust prognosticators of applicant attraction measured in later recruitment stages of application and job acceptance (Lievens, Hoye, & Schreurs, 2005). Organizational attraction precedes the decision to seek employment with an organization. Ongoing attraction influences the decision of the applicant to continue through the employment process and is an indication of how the applicant perceives the recruitment process. How the applicant is treated in the process is part of the decision-making at each stage of recruitment.

The Needs of the Applicant

The literature review focuses on three theoretical frameworks conceptualizing important factors to understand how an organization's recruitment process and practices affect the decision of an applicant to continue the recruitment process. The three theoretical frameworks include Theory of Reasoned Action (TRA), Maslow's Theory of Human Needs, and Person-Organization (P-O) fit. Candidates are seeking to satisfy a need when selecting an organization for employment. The applicant can consciously or subconsciously interpret attraction to an organization by exposure to an organizational process or representative. The theory of reasoned action (TRA) suggests that a limited set of factors can affect behavior, such as beliefs, attitudes, and behavioral purpose (Fishbein & Ajzen, 1975). This is pertinent to this study, as candidates move through the employment process were exposed to various processes and representatives of the organization. The applicant's interpretation of these interactions has been based in elements of TRA. Such interactions may influence an applicant to continue or cease progression through the employment process. Although information is incomplete, the theory of reasoned action is a method that is used by candidates to make the decision to complete the employment process.

Maslow's Theory of Human Needs has five levels in a tiered manner from lowest level needs to highest-level needs. Maslow's hierarchy of needs is: (a) physiological; (b) safety; (c) belongingness; (d) esteem; and self-actualization being the highest level (Maslow, 1943). A candidate is seeking to satisfy one or more of these needs when seeking employment. If at some point in the employment recruitment process the candidate decides these needs may not be satisfied, this revelation may influence the candidate's decision to continue or withdraw (DeGroot & Gooty, 2009).

An applicant applies the person-organization (P-O) fit theory when the applicant desires to work for an organization with similar values. Attractiveness of an organization is influenced by how the applicant perceives they will fit in the organization (Coldwell, Meurs, & Marsh, 2008). There are a number of decision points in the recruitment process where the applicant determines if an organization is a good fit. In the interview process, an applicant interacts with company representatives and this situation is a mutually beneficial interaction in that both parties determine if similar interests and values exist (Cable & Judge, 1997). The discussion for each of the theoretical frameworks reviews, analyses, synthesizes the historical and current findings and ends with a summary of key findings.

Theoretical Framework

The historical overview and current findings presented here examine three pertinent theories. The first theory is the theory of reasoned action (TRA). This theory suggests that candidates will make the decision to complete the employment process with an organization based on the interactions throughout the recruitment process (Fishbein & Ajzen, 1975). These interactions are influenced by beliefs, attitudes and behavioral intentions (Bermudez-Edo et al., 2010; Gomes & Neves, 2011). TRA proposes that potential candidates develop trust beliefs with regard to ability, integrity, and benevolence (Bermudez-Edo et al., 2010).

The TRA theory, coined by Ajzen and Fishbein (1975), was developed in 1975. Judgment formed by the applicant about organizational brand, and concerns of 'fit' with the job or the organization (Uggerslev, et al., 2012) can be influenced by interactions throughout the employment process (Bermudez-Edo, Hurtado-Torres, & Aragon-Correa, 2010). The theory of reasoned action is a subjective process (Fishbein & Ajzen, 1975). A company's website, a recruiter's demeanor and interactions, or a television commercial can influence the decision of an applicant to continue with the employment process.

Candidates take the information, no matter how incomplete, and formulate an overall impression of an organization. Theory of reasoned action (Fishbein & Ajzen, 1975) links organizational culture to recruitment activities by affecting what impressions candidates attend to; by affecting how these impressions are interpreted from data or dealings; and how such interactions can sway an applicant response and decision to complete with the employment process (Ma & Allen, 2009).

Marketing and advertising ventures convey an impression about an organization. In recruiting materials, the impression is that this organization is where you want to work. Corporate websites are filled with information to aid the applicant in the employment decision-making process. Candidates make the decision to seek employment based on the information obtained, no matter how limited.

Maslow's Theory of Human Needs states that candidates are looking to satisfy a particular need when selecting an employer. The need can be physiological, safety, belongingness, esteem or self-actualization (Maslow, 1943). An individual will fulfill basic needs before adjusting behavior to appease higher-level needs (Maslow, 1943). Individuals initially seek to satisfy physiological needs (Maslow, 1943). These are basic the human needs required to sustain life and include food, clothing and shelter. Any other needs provide little motivation until these basic needs are satisfied (Maslow, 1943).

Through the application of Maslow's Theory of Human Needs, an organization must pursue in depth what needs the applicant is trying to satisfy at work and ensure that the applicant receives the outcomes that help to satisfy those needs. If this occurs, the applicant can perform at a high level and this information can help organizations to develop recruitment plans to attract these candidates. Maslow's hierarchy of needs is described from the lowest level to the highest level: (a) physiological, (b) safety, (c) belongingness, (d) esteem, and self-actualization (Maslow, 1943). Human associations and communal needs of candidates are crucial aspects of recruitment (Maslow, 1943). Organizations must consider what the organization has to offer the applicant. Organizations must know and understand the need of an applicant when seeking to understand the concerns of candidates during the recruitment, job choice, and application process.

Physiological needs are humans' rudimentary corporal needs such as shelter, food and water. Safety needs are concerned with the belief people must feel stability and security with his or her job and this need can be affected if the applicant feels an organization is not financially stable. Information in the media concerning recent layoffs, mergers, acquisitions, corporate bankruptcy filing, and other financially based actions may trigger the applicant to be apprehensive to apply for a position with certain organizations.

Candidates use the fuzzy trace theory in processing information from the media. Cornell Professor Dr. Valerie Reyna co-developed this theory with Charles Brainerd (Brainerd & Reyna, 2002). The authors' theory involves the use of a mechanism of consistency criterion where words and actions are used to solve reasoning problems. Reyan (2004) stated the dual process theory in memory and reasoning predicts the risk perceptions of an applicant. Memory is held in a temporary store, called a working memory (Reyan, 2004). The job seeking process is influenced, where an applicant has been exposed to media information about an organization prior to instituting a job search. The exposure could be recent or could have happened years ago. Such exposure sways an applicant to seek employment with an organization or decide against applying for employment.

For instance, an applicant watches a news segment on the Hostess Brand Inc. filing for Chapter 13 bankruptcy and that the company is scheduled to close several store locations nationwide. In the segment, it was mentioned that thousands of people would lose jobs due to the closures. Years later, the applicant comes across the name of Hostess Brand, Inc. in a job search. The safety needs of an applicant are impacted based on bounded rationality from applying the working memory when exposed to the organization's name again. The applicant does not feel secure in seeking employment with Hostess, Brand Inc. Bounded rationality is not a good source of information to reflect from because of its limitations in human information processing. Hostess, Inc. can be a viable organization years later. The previous exposure to the organization through the media affected a possible employment relationship between the

62

applicant and the organization based on a compromise of the safety need. The applicant will bypass this organization in the job search.

Belongingness needs concerns the desire of an applicant to have friends, family, and intimacy, or their need to be social (Maslow, 1943). This sense of belongingness is the reason why personal interactions with business representatives (Cable & Kang, 2006) are more favorable to some candidates than messages viewed on the company website (Cable & Yu, 2006). Rich media refers to communication channels that permit timely feedback for real time exchanges of messages (Cable & Kang, 2006). This media is combined with words, facial expressions, and body posture. Research revealed participants preferred this form of recruitment interaction (Cable & Yu, 2006). To reach candidates who desire a sense of belongingness, organizations must invest time, money, and resources into face-to-face recruitment options such as career fairs, even though such forms may be more expensive than electronic job boards and websites (Cable & Yu, 2006).

In an organizational culture where everyone is out for himself or herself this creates a competitive environment where candidates feel the security of their position within company is threatened. There is no sense of belongingness. Insecure employees withhold pertinent information from peers from fear that coworkers will advance up the corporate ladder ahead of them. Sales are adversely impacted because there is no cohesiveness among employees to assist

63

customers. All of these actions affect the overall morale of employees. When the need for security is compromised, candidates can become unmotivated to pursue employment for such an employer (Hughes, Ginnett, & Curphy 1995).

Esteem needs are the desire to be appreciated, knowledgeable, and significant (Maslow, 1943). Although this need is established firmly once the applicant is hired, it can be compromised in the interview process or through subsequent communication with company employees. There are a number of opportunities where the applicant interacts face-to-face or over the telephone with the organization's representatives. A dismissive tone by a receptionist or a recruiter failing to address questions of an applicant who is considering an offer of employment may compromise this need.

Finally, self–actualization needs is the highest motivation levels (Armache, 2011) that involve individuals striving to reach all that they are capable of being (Maslow, 1943). Candidates have an attraction to organizations similar to the actual and ideal self-image of the applicant (Nolan, 2010). Candidates may not actually possess certain qualities that the applicant may expect of the organization. An applicant desires to work for an employer who has a reputation of dealing honestly and fairly with its workers. That same applicant may not deal honestly with others at all times. The applicant selects this organization as a potential employer based on its attribute of dealing honestly (Strand, et al., 1981).

Self-actualization is the most known concept coming from Maslow. Leaders must find out what needs the workforce are in search of and then make sure those needs are fulfilled. When this is accomplished, candidates perform at their highest level of productivity (Maslow, 1943). Candidates are motivated by the two levels of belongingness and esteem needs (Nolan, 2010). Once one need is satisfied, it is no longer a powerful motivator (Bateman & Snell, 2009).

The person-organization (P-O) fit theory suggests candidates match themselves with organizations that have similar values. Organizations that support various social platforms such as homelessness, recycling, poverty, literacy, or causes that support women may be appealing to those candidates who support these causes. This theory is linked to the attraction-selection-attrition (ASA) framework that suggests there is a mutual attraction between candidates and organizations based on similar values and goals (Cable & Parson, 2001; Kim, Cable, & Kim, 2005). Little research is available about how organizations can establish P-O fit during the attraction, recruitment, and the selection process.

Cable and Judge (1997) previously determined the interview process enabled both the organizational representatives and the applicant to define if the other demonstrated congruent values and interests. According to ASA, there is mutual attraction between an applicant and organization based on similarities between the two.

Judge and Bretz (1992) found there was a connection between the values of an applicant and the perceived values of the organization. Candidates who value water conservation, recycling, and other environmentally conscious processes may seek to work for organizations that participate and support such green initiatives.

Candidates who place a high priority on quality time spent with small children may seek out employers that have human resources benefits that allow the applicant to merge employment within the family structure with little disruption. Organizations often implement flexible workforce processes such as work schedule flexibility, telecommuting arrangements, on-site day care facilities, and flexible benefit plans to increase compatibility between the organization and its workers (Cable & Judge, 1997; Kim et al., 2005). This allows a family oriented applicant to maintain balance between work and family while utilizing these benefits.

Candidates, who place a high value on material possessions, associate a higher pay with the ability to acquire such possessions (Cable & Judge, 1997). For these candidates, salary is a major consideration in selecting what job or company to pursue. Compensation structures that recognize individual performance based pay is preferred over group-based pay. With individual performance as the trigger for recognition and recompense, the applicant maintains total control over pay and the ability to acquire a certain lifestyle. In a group-based pay structure, the applicant loses total control in exchange for partial contribution to performance. The employee, consequently, loses control over the results and outcomes of performance influencing compensation.

Coldwell et al. (2008) found candidates are attracted to organizations with compatible ethical values. Applicant expectations for organizations who demonstrate ethically responsible behavior has risen over the years. Ethics are included in a corporation's social responsibility (CSR). CSR is an organization's obligation to conduct business that is good for society beyond what is required of the law (Coldwell et al., 2008). CSR is also a component of an organization's reputation, which is as an attractor for employment candidates.

This study was a method of inquiry to understand the lived experiences and perceptions of candidates who voluntarily disengaged or withdrew during the recruitment employment process. Participants have also accepted an employment offer from another organization. These two requirements allowed the participants to share lived experiences and perceptions when accepting a job offer and when voluntarily disengaging during the recruitment process.

Figure 1 Steps in Decision Making Process

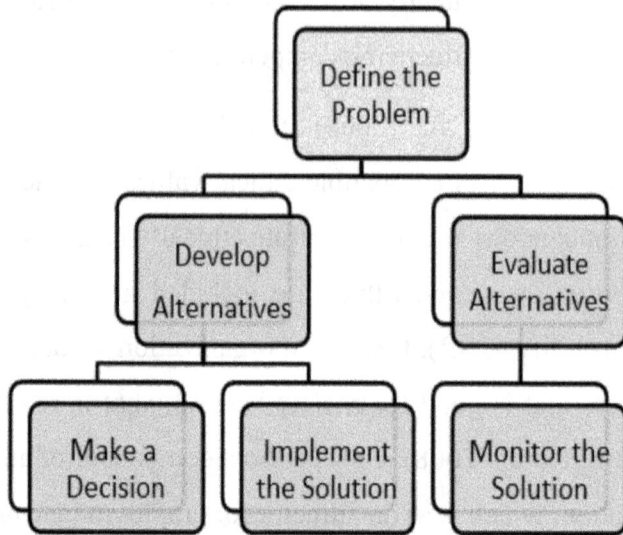

Figure 1. Steps in the decision making process illustrated from the initial step of defining the problem to the final step of monitoring the solution. Figure created by the researcher from material obtained information "6 Steps to decision-making process" by Deepa Kartha, 2012.

Once organizational recruiters recognize and understand these factors, a development plan can be created to remove or address these factors. Previous research discovered that there is a critical need to replace existing workers (Davidson, 2000) with new talent (Hurst & Good, 2009). These needed workers are recruited nationwide (Hurst & Good, 2009).

Organizations must attract (Aiman-Smith, et al., 2001), and maintain the interest of the candidate until a job offer is extended and accepted or until the employer is no longer interested in the candidate (Curran & Hyman, 2000). Failure to maintain the interest of the candidate after attracting the candidate resulted in wasted time and financial resources (Yue, 2012).

Chapter 3

Method

The purpose of this qualitative phenomenological study was to explore in depth the lived experiences and perceptions of candidates who voluntarily disengaged or withdrew from one recruitment employment process and who have accepted an employment offer from another organization. These participants were entry-level candidates with no professional work experience who were pursuing a professional career. A qualitative method was appropriate because the questioning allowed the participant to describe these lived experiences and perceptions through a personal lens of the participants within 12 months of accepting an employment offer (Mitchell, 2011).

According to Bak (2011) and Griffiths (1996), qualitative research is appropriate when there are no working models to understand the phenomenon. Past research has inquired about recruitment (Aiman et al., 2001) and organizational attraction (Walter, Wentsel, & Tomczak, 2012) in a number of studies (Salkind, 2003). There is limited research that pursues in depth the perceptions of candidates who are attracted to organizations but choose to discontinue the employment process. Recruitment activities may result in applicant attraction. This research looked a step further into when the connection was severed by the applicant prior to job offer. This study sought to understand the role the recruitment process played in a participant's decision to complete the employment process with an organization, and withdraw or disengage from the employment process of another organization.

The phenomenological research design is used when, "Research questions ask for meanings of a phenomenon with the purpose of understanding the human experience" (Crist & Tanner, p. 202). The researcher sought to understand what role the recruitment process plays in an applicant's decision to continue and discontinue the employment recruitment process. According to Vandermause (2012), phenomenology reflects an engagement in an ongoing self-showing of meaning during the question and answer process among the researcher and participant. Semi-structured tape-recorded interviews were conducted of participants. The interview sessions were approximately 60 minutes in length. The researcher interviewed until saturation was reached.

The sample size of candidates was established as sufficient to reach saturation. Sufficiency and saturation of information will determine how many participants are enough, or saturation (Seidman, 1998). Sufficiency was obtained once the researcher obtained a sufficient number of participants to reflect the range of participants and sites that made up the population (Seidman, 1998). Individuals outside the sample must be able to connect to the lived experiences and perceptions of the candidates (Seidman, 1998). Saturation of information occurred when the researcher began to hear previously heard information and at the point where the researcher is no longer learning anything new about the participants' lived experiences and perceptions of the employment recruitment process (Seidman, 1998).

The following sections elaborate on the research discussion presented in Chapter 1 regarding the research method and design appropriateness, population, sampling, and data collection and techniques to be used. Research generally originates with inquiries and expectations from the researcher surrounding a particular phenomenon (Creswell, 2007). When comprising a research study, the researcher must select a research method, and a design in which the data will be composed, examined, and understood (Creswell, 2007). The research design for this study was a phenomenological approach that consisted of semi-structured interviews where data was gathered relating to the lived experiences and perceptions of candidates seeking entry-level employment. The understanding of the role the recruitment process played in the decision of a candidate to continue and discontinue the employment recruitment process was sought.

Research Method and Design Appropriateness

Qualitative research methods are appropriate when seeking the reactions and perceptions of individuals who are experiencing a particular phenomenon (Caffarella & Barnett, 2000) and only describes that situation for that group (Caffarella & Barnett, 2000; Lowhorn, 2003). The participants for this research were candidates who had accepted at least one employment offer and had withdrawn during another employment recruitment process. Participants were interviewed about their attitudes, activities, opinions, and beliefs in the process of seeking employment (Christensen et al. 2011). The semi-structured interviews presented each participant with the same stimulus, the employment recruitment process. A qualitative research method was appropriate for this study because the researcher sought to understand the specific phenomenon of the recruitment process (Patton, 2002), which aligns to the problem and purpose statement.

A qualitative research method investigates the human condition and is focused on the individual (Watson, 2007). This method was appropriate for a study that sought to understand, by interviewing, the job search process (Patton, 2002). The research questions were written to understand the role the recruitment process played in the applicant's decision to complete the employment process with an organization and have withdrawn during another. Participants had accepted an employment offer with at least one employer and had withdrawn during the process of another employer within 12 months prior of participating in the study.

Seeking Perceptions of Individuals

Qualitative research methods are appropriate when seeking the reactions and perceptions of individuals who are experiencing a particular phenomenon to which there are no good working models (Caffarella & Barnett, 2000; Griffiths, 1996). The world is seen as a social construct with subjective meaning and intentions (Bak, 2011). The participants for this research were employment candidates. Perspectives were gathered from the participants in an agreed upon setting allowing the researcher to gain an understanding of the perceptions of the participants when going through the recruitment process to seek employment. Qualitative research methods are effective at examining human behavior in the setting in which the behavior occurs (Salkind, 2003). This qualitative study emphasized the interpretation of the data from the research.

Qualitative research was the chosen method for this study because the researcher focused on the process of decision-making and employment recruitment process completion of the participants. The researcher sought to understand the role the recruitment process played in the applicant's decision to complete the employment process. The researcher also sought to understand the role the recruitment process played in the applicant's decision to disengage or abort another employment process.

Qualitative research methods are appropriate when seeking the reactions and perceptions of individuals who are experiencing a particular phenomenon and only describes the situation for that group (Caffarella & Barnett, 2000; Lowhorn, 2003). The participants for this research had accepted at least one employment offer after actively seeking employment. The candidates were interviewed about their attitudes, activities, opinions, and beliefs in the process of seeking professional employment for the first time (Christensen et al., 2011).

The Interview as a Study Instrument

The interview was standardized to present each respondent with the same stimulus. Interviews are the most common method of data collection (Ryan & Cronin, 2007). There are specific techniques that can be used within interviews to enhance the research data: (a) the use of standardized language of distress, (b) the use of free-association structured questions, and (c) the use of projective techniques (Griffiths, 1996). Interviews are more frequently conducted face to face, but online or telephone interviews are also used (Ryan & Cronin, 2007). Face-to-face, interviews were conducted for this study to allow for follow-up questions by the researcher as needed. Semi-structured interviews were the best method for this research, as the questions encouraged conversation that led to extensive conversation, which uncovered information.

76

Research is to provide an objective account of what has been written on a given subject (Ryan & Cronin, 2007). Qualitative research follows the naturalistic paradigm based on the assumption that multiple realities exist and the research participants (Ryan & Cronin, 2007) construct such realities. Each respondent was asked the same set of questions to understand if themes existed among the collected data. The follow-up portion of the interview process allowed the researcher and participant to discuss those factors that were unique to each respondent answering the questions.

Qualitative methods provide useful tools for understanding phenomenon for which there are no working models. This method was good for answering 'why questions (Griffiths, 1996). *What* and *how* questions may also be answered using qualitative methods. One method used in qualitative research is the interview study. An interview study can take many forms. One of the most common is the semi-structured interview form (Griffiths, 1996). A semi-structured interview allowed the interviewer to deviate from the questioning when needed to pursue emerging themes or to shift the discussion back to the area of research. In a face-to-face interview, the interviewer asked participants questions and recorded the responses while probing with additional questions to clear up any ambiguities in the question (Christensen et al., 2011; Moustakas 1994).

In-person interviews offer an advantage to researchers where nonverbal communication is used to aid the researcher in the interview process (Suzuki et al., 2007). Rubin and Rubin (2005) noted the relationship developed through mutual engagement in dialogue between interviewer and participants emphasizing the humanity of both.

Challenges of Qualitative Research

Qualitative research poses a number of challenges for the researcher, specifically when dealing with emotions of interviewees (Mitchell, 2011). The researcher was prepared for some interviewees who may become emotional when discussing employment related matters. Another influence to watch out for was that a researcher's experience and background can influence the way a research project develops (Griffiths, 1996). This is known as researcher's bias (Richens & Smith, 2011).

Other Qualitative Designs Considered

Other designs considered included ethnography and, grounded theory. Ethnography and grounded theory require long-term fieldwork (Creswell, 2007). Ethnography research focuses on group behavior based on values and beliefs over a period; just as grounded theory design develops new theories based on observations over time (Christensen et al., 2011). These research designs were not suitable for this study. An understanding of the role the recruitment process played in the decision of the participant to complete the employment process during the interview eligibility period of 12 months prior to study participation was sought. This time was to be substantially shorter than the years that were required for data collection for ethnography and grounded theory. This research examined the views, opinions, and perceptions of the participants.

Research Questions

R1:   How do candidates describe their experiences regarding the method of employment application during the employment recruitment process?

R2:   What are the lived experiences of candidates regarding the interview process during the employment recruitment process?

R3:   What lived experiences did candidates describe as influencing their decision to voluntarily withdraw from the employment recruitment process?

R4:   What lived experiences influenced candidates' decision to follow through the entire employment recruitment process to job offer acceptance?

Population

Participants were entry-level candidates who were pursuing a professional position. Participants were required to have withdrawn or disengaged from a professional employment recruitment process and have accepted a job offer within 12 months of participating in the study. A professional position is defined as employment that requires prolonged course of specialized intellectual instruction, where the primary duty is performance of work where the employee will earn at least $455 a week (Professional Employees, 2014).

Interviews are by far the most common method of data collection (Ryan & Cronin, 2007). Interviews were conducted face to face (Ryan & Cronin, 2007). Face-to- face interviews were conducted for this study to allow for follow-up questions by the researcher as needed. Semi-structured interviews were the best method for this research as the semi-structured interview questions encouraged conversation, which lead to extensive conversation that uncovered information the researcher had not planned.

Sampling Frame

In qualitative research, fewer participants are chosen to give specific, in-depth information on the research topic (Griffiths, 1996). Two hundred and one prospective participants were sent emails explaining the purpose of the study and the needs of the study and were asked to indicate their interest in participating in the study.

Twenty-five responded indicating interest. Participants were selected using purposeful sampling. Participants were required to have accepted an offer of employment and have withdrawn from an employment recruitment process within 12 months' prior of participating in the study. Interviews with the participants were completed within a specified 4 to 6-week period.

The participants were selected on a voluntary basis to participate in the study. The sampling frame continued until necessary data collection and saturation were realized. All participants received an envelope with the following items: an informed consent form, an introductory letter from the researcher, and a demographic information form. The informed consent form consisted of the purpose of the study, why it is important, whom the information is for, how the information will be used, how the information will be handled, and the risks and benefits for the participant. All participants were asked to sign the informed consent form before participating in the interview. The introductory letter from the researcher included the time commitment required for the semi-structured interview and the relevant features pertaining to the context of the study. The demographic information form consisted of personal information such as age, gender, and race. Procedures for contacting potential participants were explained in the data collection section.

Informed Consent

To ensure an ethical study and protect the participant's privacy, strict procedures were followed. An invitation letter was given to each participant and the informed consent form, which included the following information: the purpose of the study, why it is important, whom the information is for, how the information will be used, how the information will be handled, and the risks and benefits for the participant. All participants were asked to sign the informed consent form before participating in the interview. Interviews consisted of four interview questions. The informed consent included the participant's written consent to audiotaping and confirmed consent for the interview to be recorded and transcribed later for research purposes. There was no videotaping as part of this study.

Confidentiality

Confidentiality involved safeguarding the names of participants from the public and protecting participants' responses so that there is no link between a specific participant and a specific response. The participant letter and informed consent form were the initial steps to ensuring confidentiality. Participants were coded numerically using Microsoft Excel. The numeric code was applied to the consent and interview documents and the consent document is filed away in a locked file cabinet. A semi-structured interview was not scheduled until a completed informed consent document was signed from the participant.

Participants who withdrew their participation after they had consented to participate in the study, notified the researcher by phone, or email using the contact information provided. If a participant withdrew participation after a completed interview, the data was destroyed and removed from the final analysis for the research study. In the event the code needed to be broken for a participant who wished to withdraw from the study after a completed interview, the file cabinet was unlocked and the coded informed consent document for that participant was located. All data for the particular code number, as well as the data of the participants, were removed from the final data analysis. All interviews began with a discussion of the confidentiality form and the along with a detailed explanation of the informed consent form, purpose of the study and a description of how the data will remain confidential.

Geographic Location

Hampton Roads is the name for the Virginia Beach- Norfolk-Newport News, VA-NC metropolitan area in southeastern Virginia, United States. Hampton Roads is notable for its large military presence and its year-round ice-free harbor, for United States Navy, Coast Guard, Air Force, NASA, Marine Corps, and Army facilities, shipyards, coal piers, and hundreds of miles of waterfront property and beaches (Top 50 Major Employers in Hampton Roads, 2013). The land area includes dozens of cities, counties and towns on the Virginia Peninsula and in South Hampton Roads. The participant interviews were conducted in Hampton Roads.

Data Collection

Moustakas (1994) describes the task of data collection as a sequence of interrelated activities dedicated to gathering quality information to respond to study research questions. A field test was conducted prior to administering the study to test the accuracy and validity of the interview questions prior to data collection.

Field test.

The field test pretesting was designed to evaluate the research study instrument, mode of data collection, and the overall accuracy of the proposed research procedures (Caspar & Peytcheva, 2011). Information for this study was collected through the interviewer-administered semi-structured interview process that involved social interaction between the field test participant and the interviewer (Griffiths, 1996).

The field test participants consisted of four individuals, two females and two males. The age range for the field test participants was diverse. The data collected from these four field test participants provided a perspective on the instrument to be used to collect data for the employment recruitment process.

The two male field test participants were college graduates who work in the field of human resources. The two female participants were employed in human resources. One female participant was a college graduate who had been employed in the field for 20 years. The second female participant was currently employed in human resources.

All four-field test participants expressed that the semi-structured interview questions were specific and detailed enough to inquire in depth what the study participants may have experienced during the employment recruitment process. One male participant commented that the interviewer would be required to use probing words or phrases frequently to encourage study participants to share needed details of their experience.

Data collection procedures.

This qualitative phenomenological study was used to discover a response to the following research questions: (a) how do participants describe their experiences regarding the method of employment application during the employment recruitment process, (b) what are the lived experiences of candidates regarding the interview process during the employment recruitment process, (c) what lived experiences did candidates describe as influencing their decision to voluntarily withdraw from the employment recruitment process, (d)

85

what lived experiences influenced candidates' decision to follow through the entire employment recruitment process to job offer acceptance? Data collection was conducted through semi-structured interviews.

In qualitative research, the focus is not on the participant, but the lived experiences and perceptions of the participant (Crist & Tanner, 2003; Griffiths, 1996). Interviews have been known to be the best tool in phenomenological research (Ryan & Cronin, 2007). The interview process allowed the researcher to ask questions and help the participant reflect on lived experiences and perceptions of seeking employment prior to graduation (Leedy & Ormrod, 2010). Previous research shows open-ended questioning, in an informal setting, helps facilitate a flexible interview atmosphere which may result in additional information into the phenomenon researched (Creswell, 2007). The confidentiality of the interview was facilitated through individual, private interviewing. Interviews continued until the researcher reached saturation.

The purpose of the in-depth interview was to acquire an understanding of the participants' experience in the employment recruitment process through how the participants' described these experiences in the research study interview (Seidman, 1998). After the interviewer received communication of a potential participant's interest in the study, the interviewer arranged a contact visit in person (Seidman, 1998) with the respondent. This interaction served as the first phase of potential participant screening. This meeting allowed the researcher to assess the respondent's appropriateness and eligibility for the study. Once the researcher was satisfied that the respondent met the eligibility criteria to participate in the study, the researcher asked the respondent to join in the study during the contact interview or got back to the respondent later (Seidman, 1998).

Instrumentation

The tests were conducted using semi-structured interviews as the instrument of research. Participants were given a narrative of the study and were asked to complete a demographic information sheet. Participants were guaranteed confidentiality of all information provided. The identity of the participants was coded and all information was locked in a cabinet throughout the study. Each respondent was presented with identical open-ended questions in the semi-structured interview.

The interviews sought to understand a participant's familiarity with various components of an organization's recruitment process such as application, employer feedback, job postings, and the interview process. The open-ended question method allowed for a more detailed response. Qualitative research seeks to explain a current situation and only describes that situation for that group (Lowhorn, n.d.). The dialogue was concluded within 1 hour for each participant. Interviews were digitally recorded and then transcribed (Ramaswami et al., 2010).

The data collection for this study was audio-taped, face-to-face, semi-structured interviews. The semi-structured interviews during this study were scheduled to last approximately 60 minutes. The total time for participating in the study ranged from 45 to 77 minutes. Interviews were conducted with each participant for the stated time or longer at the request of the participant who preferred to share extra experiences and perceptions of the employment recruitment process. All participants were asked to member check the transcript of the individual interviews for accuracy of the interview transcription.

The Role of the Researcher

The researcher serves as an instrument of data collection in qualitative descriptive phenomenological studies (Denzin & Lincoln, 2003). Data is mediated through the researcher's open-ended questioning (Seidman, 1998). The researcher's ability to write and explore the participants' lived experiences, excluding any personal biases or assumptions was critical to the reliability and validity of the data (Seidman, 1998).

The researcher performed each step of the research, data collection, and data analysis. Potential candidates for the study were recruited by email and participant referral. The researcher validated each participant's qualifications to ensure participants met the study's qualifying eligibility requirements. Informed consent was obtained from all participants. Fifteen participants agreed to participate in the research study. The researcher used field notes to document participant's non-verbal behavior during the semi-structured interview. These notes were used to determine if the behavior added meaning to the communicated lived experiences of the candidates.

An audio digital recorder was used during the face-to-face semi-structured interviews. The researcher was the sole transcriber for each participant interview. The researcher transcribed interviews were member checked by the participants for accuracy. The researcher entered interview responses in NVivo (Version 10) to analyze and code participant data. The researcher identified the emergent themes from the participant data. The researcher identified the study results and findings. The researcher stated the theoretical implications, methodological implications, and practical implication based on the responses of the candidates.

Validity and Reliability

The degree to which findings can be generalized is important. In this qualitative phenomenology study, validity and trustworthiness were critical. Trustworthiness includes the criteria of credibility, transferability, dependability and conformability (Lincoln & Guba,

1985). To increase the validity in the study the researcher interviewed the participants to collect data for the study (DeGroot & Gooty, 2009). Interviews are the most likely way to capture the lived experiences and perceptions of the participants. While interviewing, the researcher examined the body language of the participants to determine if further questions were needed to pursue in depth deeper meanings of responses (Crist &Tanner, 2003).

Data Source Triangulation

Data source triangulation was used through interviewing diverse participants about the topic of employment recruitment (Ma & Allen, 2009), and job choice decisions (Al-Hamadan, 2010). Triangulation provided a multifaceted view (Al-Hamadan, 2010). Triangulation is, 'the expansion of research methods in a single study to enhance diversity, enrich understanding, and accomplish specific goals (Al-Hamadan, 2010).

Research questions can be looked at differently using diverse methods to provide different types of responses (Griffiths, 1996). The interview questions were asked, and the order was adjusted, as needed, to describe if similar themes were reached regardless of the order in which the questions were asked (Christensen et al., 2011).

For the triangulation of data for this study, the field test included a sample of four human resources professionals. Second, the researcher conducted member checking by repeating back data to

90

field test participants their answers to ensure there was an accurate representation of information disclosed by the participant. Creswell (2007) refers to member checking as a way to increase the validity of collected data. Triangulation included candidates from the state of Virginia. The various viewpoints of the phenomena of the employment recruitment process were gathered to increase the reliability of the study findings. The third form of triangulation was the review of literature involving a number of sources and various studies about the employment recruitment process, steps in the decision making process and applicant job choice decisions. Three theoretical frameworks: (a) Maslow's Theory of Human Needs, (b) Theory of Reasoned Action (TRA), and (c) Person-Organization (P-O) *fit* were used to test theoretical triangulation using the collected data.

Data Analysis

Once the participant interviews were recorded and transcribed. The participant information was entered into NVivo10 for sorting into themes for further analysis.

Data analysis was implemented from Moustaka's (1994) data analysis:

1. List relevant experiences horizontally to ensure textual quality of participant responses, include relative

importance of the experience by the participant.

2. Eliminate immaterial or insufficient data and cluster remaining information into themes.

3. Develop a structured description of the information.

4. Create a composite of written and organized description to obtain and blend the spirit of the candidate's description.

5. Validate the themes.

The responses from the interviews were the main source of data. All participant responses to the semi-structured interviews were clustered into themes reflecting the underlying meaning of the comments (Ramaswami & Dreher, 2010). If a participant repeated an impression, it was counted one time. The responses of participants were categorized with key words representing dimension labels such as job posting, recruitment, potential employer feedback, and the interview process. When participants used the words organizations, company, companies, or employer, these words were combined together in the analysis for consistency in reporting content analysis results.

Nvivo10© software (NVivo 10, 2013) was used for this study. This software supports qualitative research methods. The software was used to collect, organize, and analyze data collected. The initial step in data analysis was for the researcher to enter information into the Nvivo10© software. Next, words and phrases that were used by the participants, that were relevant to the participants' experience, were recorded. The researcher developed meaning units for each word or phrase used by each participant.

The third step began the analytical process. This process involved the clustering of words and phrases and the creation of themes to explore the common themes among all participants. The researcher included verbatim references from the participants in the themes. During the final stage in analysis the researcher created a universal description for the participants as a group. In this stage, a general description was developed for the entire research group. The researcher used the information from the general description to present research findings.

Member checking was used to determine the reliability and validity of the data collected. The research participants were asked to review the transcribed interviews to ensure accuracy of data collected and transcribed (Ryan & Cronin, 2007). Time for the sharing of the transcribed interviews to the participants, and the return of the feedback to the researcher was incorporated in the researcher's data analysis timeline. Gibbs (2013) suggests the use of this method as a form *of respondent validation* to assessing the accuracy of the transcribed information. Five emergent themes resulted from the responses of the candidates. These were: (1) interview process, (2) discomfort during the interview process, (3) comfort during the interview process, (4) job details, and (5) person-environment fit.

Coding process

The coding process involved the use of Nvivo10© software (NVivo 10, 2013). The software aided the researcher by transcribing and recording accurately information obtained from participants (Gibbs, 2013). Data analysis for this study included the use of Nvivo10© software (NVivo 10, 2013) to pursue in depth the data obtained from the semi-structured interviews. This software was used to unite the participant information to extract themes. The use of this software removed manual tasks for the researcher involving analysis, sorting, and arranging of participant information allowing the researcher to focus of understanding and identifying trends from the data retrieved from participants (NVivo 10, 2013).

Chapter 4

Results

The purpose of this qualitative phenomenological study was to explore the lived experiences and perceptions of candidates who voluntarily disengaged or withdrew from one recruitment employment process and who accepted an employment offer from another organization. Participants in the study were candidates seeking an entry-level professional position. Participants in this study had not worked, nor had a history of working, in any professional occupation. Participants voluntarily withdrew from at least one organization's employment recruitment process. Participants also, have accepted an employment offer from another organization. These two requirements allowed the participants to share lived experiences and perceptions when accepting a job offer and when participants voluntarily disengaged during the recruitment process.

The data collection process consisted of face-to-face interviews with candidates. The purpose of this qualitative phenomenological study was to explore the lived experiences and perceptions of candidates who voluntarily disengaged or withdrew from one recruitment employment process and who accepted an employment offer from another organization. Chapter 4 includes a discussion of the research questions, data collection, participants, data analysis protocols and procedures, interview results with key word, analysis and theme identification.

Research Questions

The central research question that guided the interview questions in this study: what are the perceptions and lived experiences of candidates about the underlying reasons that led to their decision to continue or voluntarily disengaged during the employment recruitment process? The sub-questions were designed to pursue in depth connections among the employment application process, the interview process, applicant and employer communication, and the applicant's decision to continue or withdraw from the recruitment process.

R1: How do candidates describe their experiences regarding the method of employment application during the employment recruitment process?

R2: What are the lived experiences of candidates regarding the interview process during the employment recruitment process?

R3: What lived experiences did candidates describe as influencing their decision to voluntarily withdraw from the employment recruitment process?

R4:   What lived experiences influenced candidates' decision to follow through the entire employment recruitment process to job offer acceptance?

Demographic Information

The study participants were 15 candidates in Virginia. Participants included 11 females and 4 males. These participants were entry-level candidates with no work experience who were pursuing a professional career. Participants were required to have withdrawn or disengaged from a professional employment recruitment process and to have accepted a job offer within 12 months of participating in the study. Seventy-three percent of the participants were female. Twenty-seven percent were male. There were six African-American participants, six Caucasian participants, two Asian participants, and one African study participant. Participants' ages ranged from 23-30 years.

Table 1

Demographic Data for Study Participants

Participant	Age	Gender	Ethnicity
P1	26	Female	African American
P2	25	Female	African American
P3	24	Female	African
P4	24	Female	Caucasian
P5	23	Female	African American
P6	24	Female	Caucasian
P7	23	Male	Caucasian
P8	24	Female	Asian
P9	25	Female	African American
P10	25	Male	Caucasian
P11	24	Male	African American
P12	23	Female	Caucasian
P13	24	Female	Asian
P14	25	Female	African American
P15	30	Male	Caucasian

Figure 2

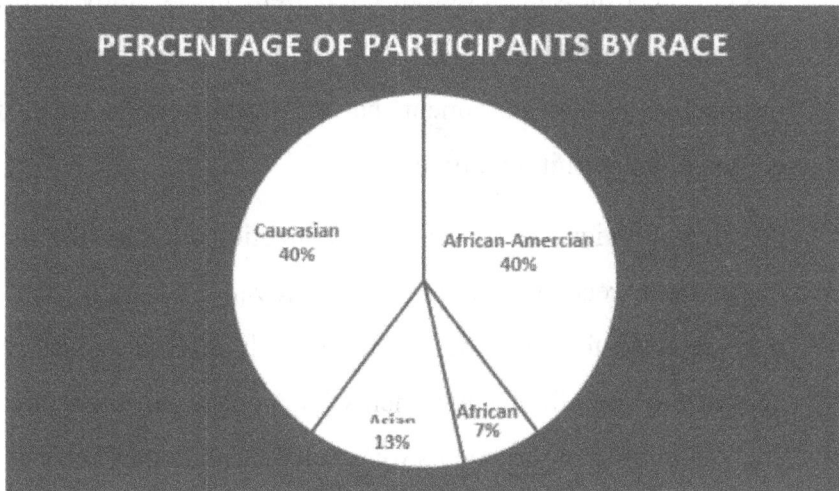

PERCENTAGE OF PARTICIPANTS BY RACE

Caucasian 40%

African-Amercian 40%

Asian 13%

African 7%

Note: This table was created from the results of the participants' responses on the demographic information sheet.

Data Collection Procedures

Field Testing was conducted to evaluate the study instrument. The field test was to assess the research study instrument, mode of data collection, and the overall accuracy of the proposed research procedures. Information for the field test was collected through the interviewer-administered semi-structured interview process that involved social interaction between the participant and the interviewer.

The field test participants consisted of four individuals, two females and two males. The field test participants were all human resources professionals and not candidates. The field test participants did not meet the same eligibility requirements as study participants. The data collected from these four field test participants provided a perspective on the instrument that was used to collect data for the employment recruitment process.

The interviewing process and collection of data for the study began upon receipt of university approval. The study participants were selected for participation in the study after each was screened against the eligibility requirements for inclusion in the study. These study eligibility requirements were that the candidates had withdrawn or disengaged from an employment recruitment process within 12 months of participating in the study. Participants must also have accepted an employment offer from another organization. These two requirements allowed the participants to share their lived experiences and perceptions when they accepted a job offer and when participants voluntarily disengaged during the recruitment process.

Information for this study was collected through the interviewer-administered semi-structured interview. To increase the validity in the study the researcher interviewed the participants to collect data for the study. The interviewer also read back the participants' responses to the participants to ensure the participants' lived experiences and perceptions were recorded accurately. Interviews are the most likely way to capture the lived experiences and perceptions of the participants. The collection of this qualitative data documented the lived experiences, thoughts, and perceptions of these participants. To obtain this number of study participants the researcher employed a number of tools to recruit participants.

Data Analysis Procedures

The data retrieved from study participants remained confidential throughout the analysis of responses. Interview responses from the candidates were entered into the Nvivo10© program by the researcher. Nvivo10© is an analysis tool used in qualitative studies that enables a researcher to group data according to phrases or words to identify themes across the framework of the study. The participant responses were coded in numerical order preceded by the letter P for participant to conceal participants' identity. Interview responses were entered under the node for the corresponding question created by the researcher. Each interview question was assigned a separate node. A node is a digital locker within the Nvivo10© program that stores documents, pictures, words, research, or videos.

Data were arranged by the corresponding questions. Responses to the four research questions of the semi-structured interviews were entered into the Nvivo10© software program under the appropriate node. Participant responses were queried for word frequency, common words and phrases for each question. Each word or phrase was calculated in the sample response percentages based on the frequency identified in the node. Participants' responses were entered into each node, which provided direct quote review and further examination of respondents' responses on the employment recruitment process.

Responses from the participants were imported into Nvivo10© software from the typed interview Word document, which aided the researcher in grouping information and identifying themes and keywords. Data was sorted according to words and phrases documented from participant responses to the interview questions. Like words, such as company and organization, were grouped under one keyword. Participant responses were entered into a node that represented the corresponding survey questions. Data saturation was recognized based on keyword frequency. Each question generated a different frequency. Data saturation level was reached at interview number 12. No new keywords emerged during interviews 13, 14 and 15. The last 3 interviews were as rich as the first 12 interviews in number of references but they did not add new perceptions or keywords to the analysis. Participant data remained confidential throughout the analysis process.

Table 2

Keyword Recognition for Data Saturation

Keyword(s)	Frequency
Job Details	16
Interview Process	10
Online	9
Email	7
Week	7
Job Fit	6
Days	5
Concerned	5
Uncomfortable	5
During	5
Comfortable	5
Benefits	4

Participant Summaries

The following summaries regarding each participant's perception of the employment recruitment process is described in detail.

Participant 1 (P1).

P1's perception of the employment recruitment process that P1 withdrew from was that of 'surprise'. P1 used the word 'surprised' when describing the telephone call received from the employer. P1 had applied for the position several months prior. It was P1's perception that the position had been filled. P1 said no acknowledgement of the employment application was provided. P1 expressed that the months elapsed from application to the telephone call was acceptable to P1 because the participant did not expect any communication from the employer because several months had already passed.

P1 mentioned that the telephone call received was not for the position P1 had applied for. Instead the call was about a lesser position. The employer inquired if P1 was interested in being considered for this lesser position. P1 attended the interview because the position was similar to the position P1 had applied for.

P1 perceived the interviewer to be impressed with the participant's credentials during the interview. However, P1 made the decision to withdraw from the employment process during the interview. P1 perceived that the interviewer felt she was not being honest when answering a question about why P1 had left a previous position. P1 stated the interviewer asked the same question three times.

As for P1's perception of the employment recruitment process to which the participant accepted an offer. P1 stated she felt confident throughout the interview. P1 stated the atmosphere of the interview made her feel like she already had the position. P1 was seeking job details in the interview. P1 said she asked a lot of questions. It was P1's perception that the interview process is easier when interviewers have some knowledge of the interviewees. P1 expressed that the interview panel members of the employment interview where she accepted an offer of employment had knowledge of P1's skills and knowledge from others.

Participant 2 (P2).

P2 applied for employment using an online application software program. P2 stated it was 3 days before she received acknowledgment of the employment application. P2 perceived the acknowledgement of her movement to the next a step in the recruitment process to be fast. P2 described that it was a week from application when she received a telephone call.

P2 described the perception of the employment interview to be very short. P2 stated that she felt like she was being pushed into the position because the interviewers offered employment and wanted P2 to start on that same day. P2 perceived the interviewers to be in a rush to hire anybody. P2 perceived this hastiness as an indication that there was something wrong in the company.

P2 described the interview process where P2 accepted an offer of employment. The experience was described by P2 as comfortable. P2 perceived the interviewers to be honest when answering questions about pay, benefits, and describing the employment recruitment process. P2 perceived the interviewers to have knowledge of P2's qualifications and background prior to the interview. P2 perceived she would be offered a position because one of the interviewers stated they wanted to hire P2. When P2 was asked by the researcher to describe the definition of 'comfortable', P2 said everyone seemed to be working together and the place felt organized. The receptionist acknowledged P2 when P2 walked into the building. In P2's opinion this felt comfortable.

Participant 3 (P3).

P3 explained the employment recruitment process for the position she accepted an offer of employment as overwhelming. P3 completed a paper application and returned the application in person. P3 stated the plan was to drop the application off. Instead P3 described an experience where P3 was directed to the director's office. P3 was given a tour of the building and offered an employment interview during this same visit. P3 was later offered the position. P3 perceived the employment recruitment process as positive, but still overwhelming due to how quickly everything progressed. P3 perceived that several of P3's friends may have vouched for P3's background and qualifications because the friends also worked for this same employer.

P3 described the employment recruitment process for the position where she withdrew. P3 said it due to a lack of job details. P3 stated the position was advertised with work hours of 9 a.m. to 5 p.m. When P3 arrived for the employment interview P3 was told the job was part-time. P3 perceived the job to be full time based on the listed work hours. P3 remained interested in the position so much so that

106

she offered to volunteer for the same position. The employer offered to allow P3 to volunteer in the gift shop, instead. The employer declined her offer to volunteer for the professional position which was advertised. P3 perceived the employment listing to be incomplete regarding the status details of that position. P3 would not have applied for the position had the position listing clearly listed that the position was part-time.

Participant 4 (P4).

P4 perceived the interview questions to be comfortable. The job requirement of late night hours was P4's perception that more would be required of P4 than simply the duties of the job. P4 expressed this schedule requirement coupled with the fact the supervisor was a male made P4 feel uncomfortable and concerned. P4 explained that her research about the position prior to the interview did not reveal this requirement of late night hours. P4 perceived this requirement to be false. At the moment of the closing handshake P4 knew she would withdraw.

In describing perceptions of the employment interview for the position where P4 accepted an employment offer, P4 described this process as comfortable and P4 perceived the interviewers to be truthful. P4 based the perception of honesty on the fact that the interviewer shared there were no advancement opportunities when asked.

Participant 5 (P5).

P5 perceived the employment recruitment process as a process with no problems. P5 applied online and received an application acknowledgement the same day. P5 described that a telephone call was received from the employer within a week of application. P5 described the perceptions of the employment process from which P5 withdrew as comfortable. P5 was comfortable with how the job was described by the interviewers. P5 described that it was at the point of the interview where the interviewers explained to P5 that employees were responsible for paying for their own retirement, that P5 decided a withdrawal from the employment process was necessary. P5 shared with the researcher that the position offer would have been accepted if the employer paid for retirement benefits.

For the position where P5 accepted an employer offer, P5 described this process by saying, "I loved it." P5 stated that as she progressed through the interview the job was everything that P5 had assumed. P5 expressed that the interviewers made the participant feel very good.

Participant 6 (P6).

P6 perceived the employment application process to be unacceptable. P6 stated that the application was submitted online. P6 received the application acknowledgement three weeks from date of application. P6 described the application process where P6 withdrew by saying there were four other candidates in the waiting room when the participant arrived. P6 perceived this to mean that the interviewers were not looking for someone in particular. P6 perceived that the employer was just looking for a body. P6 perceived the interview to be rushed. P6 made the decision to withdraw after leaving the interview.

When describing the employment interview where P6 accepted the offer, P6's perception was that the interviewers had done their research. P6 explained this to mean that the interviewers were very familiar with P6's resume. The introduction of other managers in the interview process was perceived by P6 to mean the employer cared enough about the hiring process to greet interviewees. P6 felt like part of the team due to the friendliness of the interviewers and other personnel. P6 perceived the interviewers to be prepared.

Participant 7 (P7).

It was P7's perception that had the employer been more flexible with pay, this would have prevented P7's withdrawal from the employment recruitment process. P7 perceived the pay was inadequate based on the amount of work expected. P7 stated that the interviewer expressed in the interview that the duties were a lot of work. However, the pay was not reconsidered. P7 perceived the employer to be locked into a particular pay with no consideration for a candidate's experience. P7 perceived that the employer wanted the experience but did not want to compensate P7 for that experience.

Where P7 accepted an employment offer, P7 perceived this process to be comfortable and good. P7 did not perceive any pressure during the interview process. P7 perceived the interview questions as straightforward. P7 perceived the job details described in the interview to be right in line with P7's background, training, and education.

Participant 8 (P8).

P8 applied online and within a week was scheduled for an interview. P8 interviewed with human resources personnel, the department manager and the vice president on the same day. P8 was offered the position. At the time of offer P8 had already decided to move out of state. P8 perceived the employment recruitment process to be comfortable. P8 explained had P8 stayed in the state, P8 would have accepted an offer of employment.

P8's perception of the job interviews in which P8 accepted an offer of employment was that there was room for professional growth within the company. P8 inquired about the details of the position, the benefits, and opportunities for advancement. P8 was satisfied with the answers to these inquires and accepted the offer of employment.

Participant 9 (P9).

Participant P9 perceived the employment recruitment process to be unique. P9 expressed that a job offer was given and accepted prior to completing the application in the human resources application software. P9 described the employment recruitment process as backwards due to the order of the staffing events: employment interview, employment offer, and employment application completion. Although the process was described as backwards by P9, the participant perceived the employment process to be comfortable.

P9 had completed the new hire paperwork for one job when P9 received the telephone call about another position. P9 later withdrew from the employment recruitment process. P9 explained that employer representatives informed P9 that the staffing process could take up to 4 weeks at the employment interview. By the time P9 got the call, the participant had already accepted another position. When asked what could have prevented the withdrawal from the employment recruitment process? P9 answered there was nothing that would have prevented the withdrawal. P9 was interested in both positions. It was P9's perception that an offer would have been accepted by either employer. One employer was timelier than the other, was the opinion of P9.

Participant 10 (P10).

Interviewers thought P10 was too qualified for the position. This was the perception of P10. P10 perceived the interview process went well. However, P10 stated that the interviewers expressed concern about whether P10 would be a good fit forth position. P10 explained that the withdrawal from this process resulted because P10 received an employment offer from another employer at the same time. P10

111

had not received an offer or rejection from the current employer at that time. When describing what could have prevented withdrawal from the employment recruitment process, P10 perceived that there was a mismatch regarding P10's qualifications and the job requirements of the position.

P10 described the interview process where an offer was accepted as comfortable. P10 perceived the interviewers were open. P10 expressed a *like* for how the interviewers informed P10 of the steps in the employment recruitment process. P10 expressed fondness for the two employees who P10 met during the interview process.

These individuals were employees who happened to be in the area and who wanted to meet the candidate. P10's perception of these introductions was favorable. P10 stated that information on tenure; work environment and pay were of interest to the participant. As P10 moved through the employment recruitment process it was discovered that the pay was negotiable. P10 was offered a higher pay than what was originally advertised. P10 accepted the employment offer.

Participant 11 (P11).

P11 perceived the online application program to be user- friendly, but that it required a lot of information. The position required a lot of commitment, was the perception of P11. P11 said that once the interviewers described the details of the position and the hours required, P11's feelings changed at that moment in the interview. P11 learned of this position from a posting on the internet. P11 said the required hours were not listed in the employment posting. P11 declined the invitation for a second interview. When asked what could have prevented the withdrawal? That the schedule could be negotiated, was the opinion of P11.

P11 continued participation in the employment recruitment process because the employer displayed a willingness to work with P11. It was P11's perception that the employer was willing to find a position that matched P11's qualifications. P11 was seeking job details such as the equipment used, training provided, work hours, and opportunities for advancement in the employment interview. The employer offered P11 another position, other than the advertised position. It was P11's perception that this offer was because of his skills.

Participant 12 (P12).

P12's perception of the employment recruitment process was that it was laborious and technical. A Staffing Manager left a voicemail message for P12 that said, "This is the last time I am trying to call you". It was P12's opinion that this was not true. P12 did not remember any previous messages from this manager. Once the telephone interview was completed it was P12's perception that she would never hear from the manager again. Two weeks later, P12 was offered an in-person interview.

113

A sequential interview process of multiple interviews were a bit too much, was the opinion of P12. P12 interviewed with approximately 30-32 people. The interview went from feeling very positive to feeling like it was a gauntlet in P12's opinion. It was half way through the interview that P12 made the decision to withdraw from the employment recruitment process for this position.

For the employment offer that P12 accepted, the words professional and welcoming were used by P12 to describe the perspective of this experience. P12 perceived that the interviewers recognized that interviewing is a two-way process by encouraging P12 to ask questions of them. P12 described the employment interview as a process for both parties to seek and obtain information. When P12 asked how the position impacted the organization as a whole? In P12's opinion the interviewers responded appropriately and honestly.

Participant 13 (P13).

P13 described the employment application process as annoying. It was P13's perception that employers should inform perspective candidates of the requirement to complete an online questionnaire as part of the online application process. P13 recounted an experience where P13 was forced to restart an online application process again because there was no time allotted to complete the questionnaire. P13's failure to complete this questionnaire requirement resulted in the employment application not being accepted by the employer.

Once the application was completed, it was P13's perception that employers should acknowledge applications sooner than 4 weeks. This employer took 4 weeks to acknowledge the employment application that was submitted online. When P13 was offered an employment interview it was during this interview that P13 realized that the position was different from P13's expectations. P13 withdrew from this employment recruitment process.

P13's feelings did not change throughout the employment recruitment process where P13 accepted an employment offer. P13 described the interview as comfortable. The interviewers described the position exactly how P13 thought the duties would be, in P13's opinion.

Participant 14 (P14).

P14 accepted employment in the employment recruitment process because P14 felt the position was something that the participant could grow with. P14 used the word, excited when asked about how the participant's feelings evolved as P14 progressed through the interview process. P14 described the employment interview as comfortable. Information P14 was seeking in the position interview had to do with benefits and work hours. P14 described the interview process as comfortable and relaxing.

P14 perceived another position would not be a good fit based on the position requirement of 'other duties as assigned.' Upon hearing

115

this requirement, P14 perceived the position would not be a good fit. During this interview from which P14 withdrew, the participant described the experience as awkward because P14 perceived that the bulk of the questions were being asked by P14.

Participant 15 (P15).

P15's perception concerning the employment recruitment process was that employers should list all duties relating to employment clearly. P15 perceived that employers have the ability to pile on job duties under the cover of other duties. Job postings should list all duties, was P15's opinion. P15 withdrew from an employment recruitment process where the interviewers mentioned there would be other duties' as part of the job requirements. P15 withdrew from this interview process.

When P15 perceived the posting to be clear about the job duties, P15 accepted an employment offer. When the researcher inquired if P15 had ever completed duties that were outside of the scope of the position in which P15 was employed, his response was yes. P15 did not perceive minor tasks as a problem. P15 described major duties being added to a position without additional compensation as problem for the participant.

General Themes from Participant Responses

Online Employment Application.

Many participants shared that the employment application process was online. Nine out of the fifteen study participants applied for employment using an online application process. One participant (P1) submitted an online employment application for a potential employer who was located in Richmond, Virginia, approximately 75 miles away from the participant's residence. Another participant (P7) remembered the online application process as, pretty easy and straightforward. Participant P13 recalled a questionnaire as part of the online application process. The participant was not informed about the questionnaire in advance. P13 did not have time to complete the questionnaire. The program would not let P13 advance without completing the questionnaire. P13 eventually had to start all over another time. P13 described this experience as frustrating when recounting the online application process. It was P13's perception that employers be mindful of an applicant's time when developing employment application program requirements.

Application Acknowledgement Received after a Week.

Participant responses ranged from immediate acknowledgement (P9) to 3 months (P3) to wait for employer application acknowledgement. One participant (P1) stated that the first application acknowledgement received was from an employer several months later asking if P1 was still interested in the position. The participant (P1) replied, "Yes" and was informed that the employer was calling about a different, lesser position. P1 stated to the researcher that, "I had given up on hearing from the employer."

Another participant (P10) expressed feelings of edginess because of the wait. Participant P10 shared," The employer could have at least let me know that the application was received." It was the participant's (P10) perception that she was no longer being considered for the position. Similarly, another participant (P7) shared feelings of concern about the elapsed time. The participant's feelings of not knowing prompted a question because the participant did not know the status of her application. Was I being considered? This was the concern of P7. The 2-month gap of no communication left the participant feeling uncertain.

Notification of Move to the Next Step in the Employment Process.

Several participants expressed that the extended wait of not knowing whether they were moving on in the employment recruitment process caused the participants to feel anxiety. Participant P9 was told at the interview it could take up to 4 weeks before hearing anything either way. P9 had completed the paperwork for another job when the employer contacted P9 to inform her of the pending interview. Another participant (P7) did not hear anything for 2 months. P11 disclosed it was a month before he heard about the interview because it was out of state. P11 perceived the longer the process takes, something was bound to happen to mess things up.

Interview process a factor in offer acceptance.

The interview process was cited several times in participants' responses as a factor that contributed to the participants' offer acceptance. Participant P13 liked the interview and the people interviewing. P6 expressed the perception that the interviewers seemed to have all the answers that the participant needed. Participant P12 communicated his reason for offer acceptance was that the people involved in the interview panel were professional.

Participants Seek Information.

Several participants expressed that they were seeking job details in the interview to which they withdrew. One participant (P10) sought information regarding whether the position was a long term, temporary or a contract position within the company. P10 expressed that the job listing was not specific. Another participant (P11) was looking for details of the job, equipment to be used, work hours, advancement opportunities, and if training was involved. Participant P14 was familiar with the main duties of the job and was concerned about the other duties, and hours. Participant P2 was direct and stated, "I wanted to know what I would be doing." P5 was inquiring about how long the position had been vacant. Participant P9 had a specific question about, how the position worked, and to see how different the position was compared to the processes he was aware. P9 wanted to see what type of changes would need to be made by him if he accepted this position.

Participant P1 wanted more information about what the job entailed. While another participant (P7) wanted a better understanding of the job as far as how much time was spent in different areas. Participant P12 expressed, "I wanted to know how the role of this position impacted the organization as a whole." Participant P8 inquired about the job, benefits, expectations, room for growth, and wanted to discuss where the employer saw the position evolving in 5 years. Although each participant sought varied information, all inquiries could be categorized into the theme of job details.

Interviewers made participants feel comfortable.

Study participants expressed their perceptions and lived experiences in response to the question: How did the interviewers make you feel in the interview process for which you accepted an offer of employment? Seven participants responded they felt comfortable. Participant P10 described the interviewer and people met throughout the process as very open in describing how the employment process was supposed to go and how P10 was supposed to feel throughout the process. The employer representatives made

P10 feel real comfortable as he moved through the process.

Other participants (P14, P2) felt very comfortable. P2 expressed that the interviewers were familiar with her before she walked into the room. P2 was informed that the previous interviewer had filled in the current interviewers of her qualifications. Participant P3 remembered that one interviewer kept smiling which made her feel good. Another interviewer kept saying to the participant (P3), "you will like it here." Participant P4 shared that the honesty of the interviewer made her feel comfortable. The interviewer was upfront in saying there was no opportunity for advancement. P4 appreciated this honest statement. Participant P6 felt like she was already part of the team.

More job details would have prevented withdrawal.

Eight participants shared that more information regarding job details would have prevented withdrawal from the employment recruitment process. Participant P3 expressed with disappointment that the employment ad was not clear that the position was part-time. The hours were listed 9 a.m. to 5 p.m. Participant P14 communicated that those tasks that fall under 'other duties as assigned' should have been specifically listed for candidates. Participant P13 desired more job details but expressed empathy for the employer by saying, there is only so much an employer could put in a posting description. P13 stated you cannot put a book in a job description. Participant P10 expressed, a mismatch in job fit after the interviewers described the

121

details of the job.

Decision to withdraw made during interview.

Seven participants knew during the interview process that they would withdraw from the employment recruitment process. Participant P12 was aware half way through her 10-hour interview that a withdrawal was forthcoming. P12 stated that there is a sales component involved in interviewing. P12 stated that the employer failed to recognize that interviewing was a 2-way process to determine compatibility by both the employer and the applicant. P12 arrived at her decision to withdraw from the employment process when she had to request permission to go to the bathroom in the middle of a 10-hour interview. Participant P13 expressed that she was aware during the interview she would withdraw because the responses to her questions were different from her expectations of the position. Participant P14 knew immediately upon hearing the term 'other duties as assigned' that she would withdraw. Immediately P14 knew the job would not be a good fit for her.

Participant P4 knew when she shook the interviewer's hand at the conclusion of the interview that she would withdraw. The interviewer, a male, shared that she would have to work late at night. She (P4) felt uncomfortable about this work requirement. Participant P7 shared "Half way through the interview, when the interviewers got to the scope of duties and the pay I knew I would withdraw. The pay was inadequate for the amount of work they wanted to be completed."

Participants' expressed concern with interviewers prior to withdrawal.

The role of the interviewer was significant in the participants' deciding to withdraw from the employment recruitment process. Participant P6 expressed that interviewers were not very quick to answer her questions. P6 felt like the interviewers were reading her resume for the first time at the interview. P6 shared that the interviewers failed to ask what her interests were in the company. P6 also shared that the interview was rushed.

Participant P4, a female participant, shared, "It was a male interviewer. I felt uncomfortable, like if I had accepted the job more would have been expected of me." The participant (P4) was concerned about the late hours described in the interview. P4 was familiar with the organization and had not heard of such a requirement.

Results and Findings

This section includes the results and findings from the interviews conducted with candidates who experienced the employment recruitment process. The purpose of this qualitative phenomenological study was to explore the lived experiences and perceptions of candidates who voluntarily disengaged or withdrew from one recruitment employment process and who accepted an employment offer from another organization. Participants in the study were candidates seeking an entry-level professional position. Participants in this study had not worked nor had a history of working in any professional occupation. Five emergent themes surfaced from the participants' responses.

Emergent Themes

The findings from this study contributed to establishing links between the research questions and the perceptions of the participants. Findings from the study revealed 9 general themes that materialized from participants' responses during analysis using Nvivo©10 software. First, participants applied for employment using an online employment application process. Second, participants received application acknowledgement after waiting more than a week. Third, participants expressed a delay of notification of move to next step in the employment process. Fourth, the interview process was a factor in participant offer acceptance. Fifth, participants sought more information about the job. Sixth, where participants felt comfortable with interviewers, an employment offer was accepted by the participant. Seventh, more job details would have prevented participant withdrawal from the employment recruitment process. Eighth, participants' decision to withdraw was made during interview. And lastly, where participants expressed concern with interviewers, a withdrawal resulted.

These themes were documented, reviewed, analyzed, sorted, and compared during the data analysis to present detailed descriptions of the phenomena used to answer the main research question and four sub-questions. Similar statements and words were grouped and linked to themes of a phenomenological situation. These overlapping and similar themes generated five significant themes: (1) participants cited the interview process as the reason for continuing and withdrawing from the employment recruitment process; (2) participants who experienced discomfort during the interview process withdrew from the employment recruitment process; (3) participants who experienced comfort during the interview process continued the employment recruitment process; (4) participants sought job details during the employment recruitment process; and (5) participants were seeking person- environment fit in the employment recruitment process.

Emergent Theme 1: Interview Process

The participants of the study communicated that the interview process played a large role in their decision to complete, disengage or abort the employment recruitment process. The perceptions were that if the interview process was comfortable and positive that these characteristics of comfortableness and positivity would be transferred over to the workplace in the same form.

125

The interview questions were identified by participants to be critical in the decision-making process of the participants when deciding whether to abort or continue in the employment recruitment process. Stress-based interview questions experienced by P12 had a significant effect on this participant's desire to continue in the employment recruitment process. P12 described a 10-hour stress based interview as 'torture'. Repeating the same or similar questions to participants did not contribute to participants remaining in the employment recruitment process.

Another participant P1 was annoyed at the interviewer's response to her answer to an interview question. In reviewing her resume, the interviewer inquired why P1 left a high paying position. P1 expressed that, "the job just did not work out." P1 said, "The interviewer literally expressed to me that she had a hard time believing I would walk away from that much money." From that point, P1 noticed the interview going downhill. P1 stated, "When the interviewer asked me the same question three times, I knew I would withdraw."

The duration of the interview had an impact on the participants' desire to continue in the employment process. P2 said, "I thought about how fast the interview went and basically how they were trying to get someone in the door. I got a job offer from them twenty minutes after the interview." P2 expressed that the employer frowned upon the participant's desire to provide her current employer a two

126

weeks' notice. P2 described the employment recruitment experience as, "A little unprofessional." P2 declined the employment offer. Her (P2) perception was that the employer was interested in a 'body' for the position with no consideration for the individual qualities P2 had to offer.

It was P12's perception that she would never hear from one employer again after the initial telephone interview. Later in the employment recruitment process, P12 endured a series of sequential interviews involving between 30-32 interviewers. The participant described an interview where all interviewers were asking very similar questions. It was P12's perception that she was answering the same question repeatedly. P12 described this 10-hour interview process as "laborious, technical and torture." P12 shared with the researcher that she felt the employer's actions were like they were doing her a favor by interviewing her. P12 withdrew from this employment process.

In contrast, P12 described the interview of the employment recruitment process where she accepted an employment offer as "welcoming." P12 perceived the interview to be handled professionally and felt the employer was a match from a cultural perspective based on the answers to her questions in the employment interview. This interview experience of P12 demonstrates that even when there have been a few hiccups in the employment recruitment process, not all hiccups result in the applicant aborting the employment recruitment process. Earlier in the research interview, P12 communicated to the researcher that this employer's Staffing Manager claimed to have left a number of voicemail messages for her that she did not receive. P12 shared with the researcher that the Staffing Manager had not left her any prior messages.

Emergent Theme 2: Discomfort during the Interview Process

The second theme to emerge from data analysis was that participants who experienced discomfort during the interview process were more likely to disengage or abort the employment recruitment process. The discomfort came from the behavior of interviewers and the type of interview questions asked. Also, the length of interview also caused the participants discomfort.

The behavior of the interviewers caused the participants to feel discomfort. P1 stated, two people interviewed me, a female and a male. It was very clear that the female was the one in charge. She was very dominant in the interview. The female interviewer asked why P1 left her previous employer. P1 responded it just was not working out for her. The female interviewer responded to P1 that she had a hard time believing someone would walk away from that much money. P1 perceived the interview process moving in a negative direction from that comment forward. It was P1's perception that the female interviewer perceived P1 to be dishonest in her response.

P1 further shared that she perceived that the interviewer thought that P1 had been fired or discharged. P1's non-verbal behavior describing this experience revealed a number of facial expressions. Many times P1 looked blankly at the researcher. It was evident to the researcher that P1 was experiencing some discomfort recounting this experience. After a pause during the research interview P1 expressed that she was glad when that employment interview ended. P1 made a final comment to the researcher which was, "I guess the male interviewer was there to take notes."

P2 described the behavior of her interviewers as, "A little unprofessional and too laid back. P2 felt the interviewers were not giving enough information about the job. This lack of information resulted in P2 describing a feeling of discomfort.

Another participant, P3, researched the position she applied for after submitting an employment application. Her research did not uncover required overtime in the evening hours. Her interviewer was a male. P3 perceived the male interviewer's communication of occasional evening overtime to mean she would be subjected to unwanted advances from the male interviewer. She expressed to the researcher that she felt uncomfortable. She did not accept the job offer from this employer.

Participant P4 withdrew from the employment recruitment process where in the employment interview the male interviewer informed P4 of required evening working hours. P4 shared that she had been interviewed by male interviewers before. P4 stated that she researched the position prior to the employment interview. P4's research did not reveal evening work hours. This revelation made P4 feel uncomfortable. P4 withdrew from this employment recruitment process.

It was the perception of participant P6 that the employment interview was, "a bit off." P6 stated the interviewers were not very clear about the requirements for the position. P6 expressed that the interviewers could not give her information about the actual position she was interviewing for. P6 interpreted this lack of information to mean she would not get answers to her questions if she worked for the employer.

P6 recalled that, "the demeanor of the whole place was wrong." When asked to elaborate on the statement, P6 recalled that upon entrance to the facility she was not properly greeted. This omission to greet the applicant left P6 with an undesirable impression as she entered the interview.

Another observation from the interview expressed by P6 was that it was her perception that the interviewers were reviewing her application and resume for the first time in the interview. When interviewers were not quick to answer P6's questions in the employment interview, P6 decided she would withdraw from the employment recruitment process. P6 shared with the researcher that there were four other candidates in the lobby waiting to be interviewed when she exited the room where the interview took place. P6 interpreted their presence to mean that the employer was not looking for a specific skill set, just a 'body.

P10 withdrew from an employment recruitment process where in the interview P10 perceived that the interviewers underestimated P10's job knowledge. P10 expressed discomfort during the interview when the interviewers expressed they were unsure if the position would be a good 'fit' for P10.

Participants expressed that certain factors involving interview questions caused discomfort in the interview process. P13, stated, "I could tell by the way the questions were going that the job was not something I really wanted. The interview questions asked, can give insight into the job." Repetitiveness of interview questions caused participants discomfort during the employment interview process. It was the perceptions of the participants that the interviewers did not believe the answers given in response to the interview questions.

The duration of the interview was cited as a reason for discomfort by several study participants. P12 described a 10-hour stress-based interview process involving 30- 32 interviewers as "laborious, technical and torture." P12 shared that all of the interviewers were asking questions of P12. Some of the interviewers were asking the same questions. P12 stated she was continually answering the same questions. P12 stated to the researcher that she perceived the interviewers felt like they were doing her a favor by interviewing her.

131

P2 expressed concern regarding an interview short in duration. P2 said, "The interview was short. I felt like they were trying to push me into the position. They wanted me to start on the same day as the interview. They did not want to give me time to reflect and see how I felt about the job. I felt uncomfortable." P2 perceived the employers hasty job offer as a sign of possible internal turmoil. Participant P14 perceived an employment interview to be uncomfortable where P14 was asking more questions of the interviewers than the interviewers of P14.

Emergent Theme 3: Comfort during the Interview Process

Another theme that emerged from the data analysis was that participants who experienced comfort during the interview process were more likely to continue in the employment recruitment process. Participants expressed that interviewers must be honest and informative about the employer and the position. A common response from participants was that the behavior of the interviewers set the tone for the overall interview. All participants who continued in the employment recruitment process mentioned that they felt comfortable with the interviewers, the interview questions, or the entire interview process. P2 explained, "They met my standards. Everything I was looking for was in that job. I felt comfortable."

P10, stated, "The interviewer, as well as people I met throughout that process, were very open regarding how things were supposed to go and how I was supposed to feel. They made me feel real comfortable as I moved through the process." Participant P10 expressed that when interviewers described the employment recruitment process, step-by-step, P10 felt comfortable about the interviewers being up front about how things were going to progress. P10 expressed that she had a feeling about how things would move through the chain and she comfortable knowing who she would talk to throughout the process.

Participant P1 felt comfortable in the employment interview because she had previously worked with some of the interviewers in another facility. Interviewer behavior resulted in P1 feeling comfortable during the employment interview. P1 experienced comfort because the interviewers were talking to P1 as if she had the position.

Another participant, P3, experienced comfort in her employment interview. P3 recalled one interviewer repeatedly saying in the interview, "we really want you." P3 shared that mutually acquainted individuals had shared P3's qualifications and experience prior to P3's interview. P3 shared with the researcher that she remembers thinking in the employment interview, "you heard, heard from who?" The non-verbal behavior of smiling aided P3 in feeling comfortable in the interview process. P3 shared that one interviewer smiled throughout the employment interview.

P7 felt comfortable during the interview process because P7 did not feel any pressure. P7 communicated to the researcher that the questions were not difficult, tricky, or subjective. P7 perceived the interview questions to be straight forward. P7 shared that the employment interview questions were behavioral type questions about past experiences and how P7 would handle future such experiences. P7 accepted an employment offer from this employer.

Participant P14 shared, "It was one interviewer. It was very comfortable." They kind of knew a little bit about me before I walked into the room..." P4 echoed the sentiments of other participants, "They made me feel comfortable. The interviewer was upfront in saying there is no advancement and I appreciated that." Participant P8 stated, "I was comfortable."

Emergent Theme 4: Job Details

The term job details surfaced in its exact form, or a derivative of the term in participants' responses regarding why the participants continued or withdrew from the employment recruitment process. In response to what could have prevented participants from disengaging from the employment recruitment process, job details were expressed by participants specifically. Job details were communicated indirectly by responses of job hours (P11), benefits (P5) and compensation (P7).

Participants shared that it was the job details that resulted in the participants' withdrawal from the employment recruitment process.

P11 stated, "Once they described the details of the job, I knew it was not going to work because I have a family." It was P11's perception that the required work schedule would be disruptive to P11's family time. P14 expressed, "Some of the requirements of the job concerned me." Another participant, P4, stated, "After they gave me all of the ins and outs of what the job entailed. I felt uncomfortable about the job." And P7 shared, "Once I heard the scope of the job and the pay for the job I was not interested."

Another participant, P6, expressed it was the employer representative's inability to provide job details about the position in the interview that resulted in P6 withdrawing from the employment recruitment process. For P9 the details of the job were the deciding factor of whether P9 accepted employment. P9 wanted experience in the duties required for the position P9 accepted. As a result, P9 withdrew from the employment recruitment process of another employer. It was P9's perception that the accepted offer was a better fit for P9 then the rejected employment offers.

In contrast to those who aborted the employment recruitment process due to job details, other participants continued because of the details of the job. Participant P5 found the independent nature of a position she was interviewing for to be desirable. P5 shared, "I like my privacy. I would have my own office. I am not my own boss, but I can pretty much do what I want to do. I don't have anybody working over me." P7 said, "The job itself was right in line with my

135

background, training, and my degree. That kept me engaged in the process."

Emergent Theme 5: Person-environment fit

The final theme that emerged during data analysis was that the participants were assessing person-environment fit throughout the employment recruitment process to determine whether to continue or withdraw from the employment recruitment process. Throughout each stage of the employment recruitment process, participants' evaluated whether to continue or disengage based on activities in the employment recruitment process that had transpired up to the point of the decision. The evaluation of job details, job hours, employer benefits, and compensation are all factors participants' evaluated to determine person-environment fit based on the participant's needs. P1 asked the following questions of the potential employer to determine person-environment fit. P1 asked, "What will I be doing? What are your expectations? How are the people in the position currently interacting?"

Participant P12 inquired, "How does the role of this position impact the organization as a whole? And how will my skills would be further developed by taking this job." Inquiries about professional training and development were common from those candidates evaluating person-environment fit. When candidates could not determine if a position was a person-environment fit it resulted in a withdrawal from the employment recruitment process. Participants' decision to withdraw was made during interview. And lastly, where participants expressed concern with interviewers, a withdrawal resulted from the employment recruitment process. From the nine (9) initial themes, five (5) emergent themes were identified.

Participants cited the interview process as the reason for continuing and withdrawing from the employment recruitment process. Participants who experienced discomfort during the interview process withdrew from the employment recruitment process. Participants who experienced comfort during the interview process continued the employment recruitment process. Participants sought job details during the employment recruitment process. Participants were seeking person-environment fit in the employment recruitment process.

The study participants described the employment interview process as being instrumental in their decision to continue or abort an employment recruitment process. The lived experiences and perceptions of the candidates revealed that the participants were seeking job details information from the employer to which the participant aborted the employment process and the employer to which the participant accepted a job offer. Participants shared their experiences regarding the application process, the employment interview, the interviewers, and follow-up throughout each stage in the employment recruitment process. Chapter 5 will consist of the research findings implications, theoretical framework implications, methodological implications, limitations, and recommendations for future study.

Chapter 5

Conclusions and Recommendations

The purpose of this qualitative phenomenological study was to explore the lived experiences and perceptions of candidates who voluntarily disengaged or withdrew from one recruitment employment process and who accepted an employment offer from another organization. Fifteen candidates participated in this study. The results of the study identified the interview process as the prominent factor in the employment recruitment process. The interview process was cited by participants as the reason for the continuation in the employment recruitment process and the reason for participants aborting or withdrawing from the employment recruitment process.

Chapter 4 contained the results of the participant interviews conducted with the 15 candidates currently seeking full-time professional employment. Chapter 5 presents a discussion of the results explored in Chapter 4 of the candidates' responses and perceptions when experiencing the employment recruitment process while seeking employment. Chapter 5 also presents a discussion of the results as they relate to the theoretical frameworks for this study which include Theory of Reasoned Action (TRA), Maslow's Theory of Human Needs, and Person- Organization (P-O) Fit Theory. Chapter 5 also includes recommendations for College Career Services personnel and employers.

Research Study Problems and Questions

Despite ongoing recruitment on college campuses, not all candidates complete the employment recruitment process once initiated by the graduate. The Bureau of Labor Statistics estimates that over the 2012-2022 decade there will be 50.6 million job openings to be filled (United States Bureau of Statistics, 2012). The general problem for this study was there will not be enough qualified candidates to fill vacant positions over the next 10 years, as projected by the Bureau of Labor and Statistics.

The employment recruitment process is the origination to satisfying these labor projections. Candidates have the recent skill-set and current knowledge that employers are seeking (Aiman-Smith, et al., 2001). The employment recruitment process is used by employers to fill these needed positions. The central question for this study was, what are the perceptions and lived experiences of candidates about the underlying reasons that led to their decision to voluntarily disengage, withdraw or continue in the employment recruitment process?

This study included four research questions that focused on the lived experiences of candidates seeking professional employment for the first time.

The guiding research questions for this study were:

R1:   How do candidates describe their experiences regarding the method of employment application during the employment recruitment process?

R2:   What are the lived experiences of candidates regarding the interview process during the employment recruitment process?

R3:   What lived experiences did candidates describe as influencing their decision to voluntarily withdraw from the employment recruitment process?

R4:   What lived experiences influenced candidates' decision to follow through the entire employment recruitment process to job offer acceptance?

Responses by the study participants to the first research question revealed that sixty percent of the study participants applied for employment through an online application process. Participants expressed approval of the convenience of using an online application program from any computer as desirable. Participants also enjoyed the convenience of submitting employment applications outside of the traditional office hours of 9 a.m. to 5 p.m.

141

Participants waited more than a week before receiving application acknowledgement from the potential employer. Many of the participants found this time frame to be unacceptable. Some participants expressed confusion in understanding the delay. It was the perception of some participants that employer online application software would be immediate when it comes to application acknowledgement.

The time from submitting the application to contact from the employer reported by study participants, ranged from one day to several months of no communication from the employer after application. This time frame was an important finding by the researcher. The lived experiences and perceptions of the study participants during this time uncovered emotions of disinterest as time went on, to feelings of edginess and uncertainty due to the wait. Although only one participant expressed an immediate employer acknowledgement, several other participants expressed that an immediate response would be the preferred time frame of application acknowledgement for online application software programs.

Responses by the study participants to the second research question revealed the impact of the interview in the employment recruitment process. Each of the 15 study participants (100%) experienced interaction in the interview process that facilitated the participants' decision to continue or withdraw from the employment recruitment process. The data analysis revealed ninety-nine percent of the participants expressed that the interviewers made the participants feel uncomfortable during the interview process from which the participants withdrew or aborted the employment recruitment process. One participant (P1) expressed discomfort when an interviewer repeatedly asked the same question in a slightly different form. Another participant (P12) was visibly shaken while describing a 10-hour stress based interview where the participant felt forced to seek permission to use the bathroom midway through the interview process. In contrast, participant P14 described the interview experience as awkward when she realized that more questions were being asked by her, than from the interviewers.

In contrast to these results, forty percent of the study participants expressed that in the interview where interviewers made the participants feel comfortable, participants later accepted a job offer from this employer. Responses from the participants revealed that it was during the interview process they were seeking information such as job details, benefits, and training opportunities for advancement. Fifty-three percent of study participants stated they were seeking job details information in the interview process from which the participants withdrew. Twenty-seven percent of participants cited they were seeking job details information from the interview from which the participants accepted an employment offer. The interview was identified by participants as acritical factor in the employment recruitment process. Fifty-three percent of the participants shared that it was during the interview the participants knew they would withdraw from the employment recruitment process due to some factor involving the interview.

Responses by the study participants to the third research question revealed that candidates shared, as a result of their lived experiences and perceptions that the employment interview influenced their decision to withdraw from the employment recruitment process. Several factors cited by the study participants were elements of the interview process. The type of interview used by an employer was communicated by one participant. A ten hour, sequential interview with multiple interviewers involving 30-32 interviewers was cited as torture by one participant. The type of interview questions selected by the panel interviewers were described as uncomfortable for several participants. In contrast to the previously mentioned 10-hour interview, a significantly short in duration interview was shared as uncomfortable for a participant even though a job offer was extended at the conclusion of the interview. Stress-based interview questions were described by one participant as unwelcome.

During the interview, participants articulated that it was the details of the job shared by employer representatives during the interview that played an integral part in the participants' decision to continue or withdrew from the employment recruitment process. Information regarding the job details, benefits, training, and job schedules were all communicated by employer representatives in the interview. This information was revealed as instrumental in the participant decision-making to continue or abort the employment recruitment process. In response to research question four, it was the employment interview that influenced forty percent of study participants to continue in the employment recruitment process and accept an employment offer. Also, it was thirty-three percent of study participants who expressed it were the position fit as it was described in the interview that influenced the participants to continue in the employment recruitment process.

Discussion of Findings

This study contributed to the literature base regarding the retention of candidates in the employment recruitment process. The findings allowed the researcher to provide recommendations for existing employers focused on the retention of employment candidates. A discussion of themes is important to explore the recommendations in detail. The study survey instrument allowed participants to respond to the open-ended questions openly and honesty. Participant responses revealed that the interview process was instrumental in the participant's decision to continue or abort the employment recruitment process. Five emergent themes resulted from the participant responses to the interview questions. Participants cited the interview process as the reason for continuing and withdrawing from the employment recruitment process.

Participants who experienced discomfort during the interview process withdrew from the employment recruitment process. Participants who experienced comfort during the interview process continued the employment recruitment process. Participants sought job details during the employment recruitment process. Participants were seeking person- environment fit in the employment recruitment process.

Emergent Theme #1: Interview Process

The lived experiences and perceptions of the participants revealed that the interview process is critical in the applicant's decision to continue or disengage from the employment recruitment process. Several factors of the interview process were cited by participants. Nonverbal cues by the interviewer, such as smiling, resulted in a participant feeling comfortable during the interview. The participant later accepted an employment offer from the same employer. This reaction was linked to a study by (DeGroot & Gooty, 2009) where researchers found dynamic cues such as smiling or gesturing is perceived to be more extraverted and sociable in the employment interview. Research has made a distinction between genuine and false smiling. False smiling was found to result in a less favorable evaluation (Macan, 2009).

The type of interview was referenced by participants as a reason for continuation or disengagement. Eighty-percent of the participants experienced panel interviews. All participants of this study who accepted an employment offer, did so after participating in a panel

146

interview. Research revealed human resource professionals have had favorable perceptions of panel interviews (Macan, 2009). There is limited research documenting an applicant's reactions to panel interviews. In contrast to the panel interview that consists of two or more members, the emotional response of one female participant to a one-on- one interview with a male interviewer resulted in fear that more would be expected of her than the job required due to a requirement to work evening hours. Walker (2011) found that smaller organizations generally have one person interviewing, while larger organizations use search firms or panel interviews.

Another participant experienced a ten-hour stress based interview that was described as 'torture'. This interview was cited by the participant as the reason she disengaged and aborted the employment process. Macan (2009) found that situational and behavior based interviews required further research to enhance validity and reliability of interviewer's judgements and differences in how the interview is conducted.

Another element of the interview process cited by participants was the duration of the employment interview. Participant responses revealed that a short interview is viewed unfavorably. In contrast, a ten-hour employment interview was seen similarly unfavorable.

The behavior or actions of the interviewers was mentioned as a reason for the participant to continue or abort the employment recruitment process. Participant P7 liked the professionalism of the

147

interview panel members. This was P7's reason for accepting an employment offer from the employer. Where participants described the interviewers as comfortable, the employment recruitment process more likely resulted in an offer acceptance by the participant. Study participants expressed honestly from interviewers as favorable even if the answer was not what the participant wanted to hear. Where interviewers were described as slow to answer participant questions, the applicant interpreted this delay as a sign of dishonesty, indicative of the interviewer and organization.

These findings are important to employers who are engaged in the recruitment process. Employers must refine and enhance every step throughout the employment recruitment process. Study participants commented on the duration of the employment interview, the interview questions, and the verbal and non-verbal behavior of interviewers. Arbitrarily approaching the interview process without review and planning each element may result in the withdrawal of a qualified candidate. Study participants responded that the interview process was the reason the participant continued and withdrew from the employment recruitment process.

Emergent Theme #2: Discomfort during the Interview Process

Fifty-three percent of study participants expressed concern throughout the interview process from which they withdrew. In April 2013, Talent Q conducted a survey of 526 college graduates and undergraduates, asking them about their experience of applying for jobs. The results of the study were that four flaws in the employment recruitment process frustrated participants. These areas were lack of communication, duration of selection process, behavior of interviewers, and finding out that the position was different from what was advertised ("Through the eyes" *TalentQ*, 2013). The results of this study revealed that the study participants' lived experiences and perceptions were identical to the findings of the 2013 study. Job details were cited by this study's participants as the information participants were seeking most in the employment interview.

Employment interviews are the most common selection devices used by organizations (McCarthy, Iddekinge, & Campion, 2010). Rubin and Rubin (2005) noted a relationship develops through mutual engagement in dialogue between interviewer and candidate. Ninety-nine percent of study participants stated that the interviewers made them feel uncomfortable throughout the interview process from which the participants later decided to withdraw. Behavior of interviewers was reported as one of four flaws in the employment recruitment process ("Through the eyes" *Talent Q*, 2013). One participant described a ten hour, stress-based interview as 'torture' when responding to an interview question. Eighty percent of the study participants reported panel interviews were the chosen interview method for employers. Research continues to examine a variety of issues related to panel interviews (Macan, 2009). Some candidates expressed uncomfortable perceptions of various interview

149

panel members. Forty-seven percent of study participants stated they knew at the point of the employment interview that they would withdraw from the employment recruitment process. Factors that contributed to participants' withdrawal were: repetitive interview questions, extended length of employment interview, short duration of employment interview, perceived dishonesty of interviewers' panel statements, and incompatible job details. These findings are important to the body of knowledge because the interview process was cited as the reason for study participants continuing and aborting the employment recruitment process.

Emergent Theme #3: Comfort during the Interview Process

Forty percent of the study participants stated that some action within the interview process was the reason the participant continued in the employment recruitment process. Participants expressed that they felt comfortable throughout the employment interview to which the participant accepted a job offer. Carless & Imber (2007) wrote that interviewers have an indirect effect on applicant attraction. The authors revealed that interviewer characteristics affect an applicant's perception of a job and an organization. One study participant replied favorably in response to an interviewer who smiled at her throughout the interview. Another participant recounted the honesty of an interviewer who shared the position that she applied for did not have opportunities for advancement. The participant appreciated the honesty, although the answer was not the participant's desired response.

These findings are important to the body of knowledge because employers must continue to utilize those actions that make candidates feel comfortable to continue throughout the employment recruitment process. Employers need to fill the anticipated million positions anticipated to be vacant in the 2012-2022 decade (United States Bureau of Statistics, 2012). The loss of one qualified applicant can impact operations if a comparably qualified applicant is not secured quickly.

Emergent Theme #4: Job Details

Fifty-three percent of study participants stated they were seeking job details in the employment interview from which they withdrew. Generally, employment candidates pursue employment after responding to a job ad. Participants expressed that these ads lack extensive information about the job. This omission of information required that candidates ask more questions about job details throughout the employment recruitment process.

Participants stated that more job details would have prevented the participant from withdrawing from the employment recruitment process. Cooman & Pepermans (2012) wrote that employers who communicate the right information about positions in job advertisements will benefit financially in that candidates are well

151

informed in the initial stages of the employment recruitment process. In contrast, twenty-seven percent of study participants stated they were seeking job details information in the interview which they accepted an employment offer. These findings are important to the body of knowledge because job details are important to all candidates. Exposing candidates to job details early in the recruitment process eliminates company representatives from wasting time communicating or interviewing candidates who may not complete the employment recruitment process.

It was participant's P10's perception that the job details of the position to which P10 was interviewing for and P10's qualifications did not match up. P10 discovered this after several interview questions during the employment interview. Although it was P10's perception that the interviewers believed there was a match, P10 withdrew from this employment recruitment process. Another participant P11 withdrew from the employment recruitment process after learning the job hours for the position.

P13 understood employers may have difficulty when trying to list all relevant information of interest to candidates. It was P13's desire to gain additional job information in the employment interview. Unfortunately for P13, the interview is where P13 learned that the position that she was interviewing for required work hours that were in conflict with P13's family obligations.

The experience of participant P14 revealed that every task of a position is relevant to the applicant. Upon learning that the position that she was interviewing for was required to set-up luncheons, P14 withdrew from the employment recruitment process. Another participant P3 experienced the revelation that job listings should include the status of a position. A position's schedule was listed as 9 am to 5 pm. It was revealed in the employment interview to be part-time instead of full-time as P3 assumed. The details of part-time or full-time would have eliminated candidates such as P3 from applying who were seeking a full-time position. P5 was seeking an employment opportunity were the employer paid for retirement benefits. Upon learning in the employment interview that retirement benefits were paid by the employee, P5 withdrew from the employment recruitment process. Participant P7 was seeking an employment opportunity where hiring managers have flexibility to offer compensation based on experience. P7 withdrew from an employment recruitment process where the hiring managers were locked into a starting pay with no consideration for the qualifications of the applicant.

Emergent Theme #5: Person-Environment (P-E) Fit

P-E Fit is commonly used for the selection and recruitment of new employees (Carless & Imber, 2007). The category of person-environment fit is matched to three forms: person-job fit, person-organization fit, and person-group fit (Suptan 2011). Participant P11 gave the reason of person-job fit for her withdrawal from the employment process. She knew when the interviewer shared the number of hours required to complete the job that the schedule would adversely impact quality time with her family.

Another participant P12 equated the ten-hour sequential stress based interview as a representation of a company culture that she did not want to work for. This analysis by the participant can be categorized as person-organization fit. Several participants cited job details of: duties, schedule, and organizational reporting structure as reasons for the participant withdrawal from the employment recruitment process. Participant P10 stated once the interviewer described the details of the position that she knew the position was not going to work for her. The job required too many hours was the perception of P10.

Person-job fit was cited by P13. Participant P13 recalled it was the interview questions which gave her an indication that the position was not a position she really wanted. It was P13's perception that interview questions can give a candidate insight into the requirements of the position. It was also P13's perception that job postings should contain as much information about a position as possible. P13 shared, "Employers cannot put a book in job postings" however it was still P13's position that employers could do a better job of including information in employment advertisements. Another participant P14 voiced a similar concern recalling the interview where she heard the phrase, 'other duties as assigned'. It was P14's experience that positions that associated with this requirement were undesirable to her.

It was the interviewer's perceived dishonesty that influenced P2's decision to withdraw from the employment recruitment process. P2 shared that the interviewer offered her more money to start immediately. This gesture caused P2 to perceive that the interviewers were withholding information regarding the status of the company.

Participant P4 shared it was the position schedule that influenced her decision to disengage from the employment recruitment process. The position required that P4 work late night hours. P4 perceived this requirement to be undesirable. Participant P7 described the compensation and the scope of the position duties as the reason for withdrawal from the employment recruitment process. P7 also expressed a concern about the position that the job reported too.

In contrast, participant P1 decided to accept an offer of employment after an interview, and tour of the facility. The participant concluded both person-job fit and person-organization fit were compatible to her employment requirements. Similarly, P13 enjoyed the interview experience so much that P13 decided to accept the employment offer, if offered, even though P13 did not know a lot about the position. P13 simply liked the interviewers and that was enough for the participant.

Another participant, P11, was impressed that the interviewers offered him a higher grade position after hearing his skills and

155

qualifications. This gesture was illustrative of a person-organizational fit to which he wanted to be included. The participant received an employment offer to which he accepted. These findings are important to the body of knowledge because employers must be aware that candidates are evaluating P-E fit throughout every stage in the employment recruitment process.

Implications of the Research Question Findings

This section provides a discussion of the connection between theoretical frameworks and the results and recommendations of this study. Throughout the discussion, the researcher provides a description of the findings and their relation to past studies conducted by previous researchers in employment recruitment. The following discussion provides the researcher's perspective on the theoretical, methodological, and practical implications of this study.

Theoretical Framework Implications

For this descriptive phenomenological study, the majority of the candidates participating in the study perceived the employment interview process to be the influencing factor when deciding to continue or abort the employment recruitment process. The theoretical implications from the research findings are addressed as follows.

Theory of Reasoned Action (TRA).

This philosophy is relevant to this study because the theory advocates that there are three elements of human behavior intents: (a) attitude towards a behavior, (b) social pressure to engage in certain behavior, and (c) personal and moral norms (Fishbein &Ajzen 1975). Findings reported in this study were consistent with this theory. Study participants made the decision to continue or disengage in the employment recruitment process as a result of the participants' interactions throughout the process. Participants' attitudes towards the employer representatives' behavior influenced the decision of the candidate to continue or disengage in the employment recruitment process.

A second finding in the study consistent with the literature was that candidates develop trust beliefs with regard to ability, integrity, and benevolence (Bermudez-Edo, et al., 2010). Participants expressed feeling uncomfortable when they perceived interviewers were not being honest when answering questions. This theory advocates that when candidates are confronted with certain behaviors, the applicant will use that experience to make an overall impression of the representative, the job, and the potential employer. Study participants withdrew from the recruitment process as a result of these perceptions of dishonesty.

157

Additional findings were consistent with the review of literature. Study participants who experienced a lengthy interview were uncomfortable; likewise, a participant who experienced an interview unusually short in duration was also uncomfortable. Both participants withdrew from the employment process as a result of their perceptions about the duration of the interview. The theory links applicant perceptions with applicant behavior (Fishbein & Ajzen, 1975) in the employment recruitment process. Although participants had varying perceptions of the interview, the applicant's decision, as a result of the interview, was withdrawal.

Participant interviews revealed that candidates responded to interaction from employer representatives during the employment process. This interaction resulted in the participant continuing or disengaging from the employment recruitment process. The literature states that TRA is a very subjective process. An applicant will use any information available, no matter how incomplete, to formulate a perception. The findings in this study were consistent with the review of literature on the theory of reasoned action. These findings are important because employers must be aware that any element of the recruitment process can be a factor that causes the applicant to withdraw from the employment process. Candidates do not have to consider the entire employment process when making decisions to continue or abort the employment recruitment process.

Maslow's Theory of Human Needs.

This theory has five levels in a tiered manner from lowest level needs to highest-level needs (Armache, 2011; Maslow, 1943). Maslow's hierarchy of needs are: (a) physiological needs (Maslow, 1943); (b) safety needs; (c) belongingness needs (Maslow, 1943); (d) esteem needs; and self-actualization needs being the highest level (Maslow, 1943). Each one of Maslow's needs in the hierarchy relate to fulfilling the intrinsic or extrinsic needs of an applicant (Maslow, 1943).

Intrinsic needs are internal desires to perform a task, which gives an applicant pleasure (Maslow, 1943). Extrinsic needs are factors external to the applicant for example compensation or benefits (Maslow, 1943). The participants used elements of Maslow's theory of human needs when selecting a prospective employer based on the applicant's awareness that a particular need must be fulfilled.

The research findings from this study support this theory. Participants utilized a matching criterion when selecting potential employers. This was expressed when participants articulated why the decision was made to continue or disengage from an employment recruitment process. When the participants were informed that the job details were different from their requirements, the participant disengaged from the process. Where the participants were satisfied with the answer received from the employer, the participants were more likely to continue in the employment recruitment process.

Job details were an emergent theme from this study. One hundred percent of the study participants expressed directly or indirectly they were seeking more information about the job in the interview process. These details were: (a) location of the position, (b) schedule, (c) advancement opportunities, (d) training opportunities, (e) benefits, (f) cultural fit, and (g) duties of the position.

An applicant is consciously or subconsciously attempting to satisfy an intrinsic or extrinsic need by the continuation in the employment recruitment process. Study participants in this research revealed they were seeking information in the interview process. Such factors are those elements that a candidate examines to determine if extrinsic needs will be met by this employer. A review of the literature reveals that rarely do individuals reach the fifth level of self-actualization (Maslow, 1943). Self- actualization is a growth need which will be an ongoing need as people age. The first four needs are deficiency needs. The desire comes from those things we are lacking and can be acquired from others.

These findings are important to the body of knowledge because employers must recognize that candidates are attempting to satisfy a need when seeking employment. The findings reveal that once qualified candidates determine they have the qualifications for a position. The applicant must then evaluate the position and the employer. An applicant must then determine that by accepting the position, the applicant's needs will be met.

Person-Organization Fit Theory.

According to the person-organization (P-O) fit theory, candidates are attracted to organizations that have similar values as the applicant (Cable & Judge, 1997). Research shows that there is mutual attraction between an applicant and organization based on similarities between the two (Coldwell, et al., 2008). Judge and Bretz (1992) found that there was a connection between ethics of an applicant and the applicant's perceived ethics of an organization. Study participants expressed feeling uncomfortable when they perceived the employment interviewers were not being honest.

Similarly, participant P3 withdrew from an employment interview process where interviewers asked P3 a similar interview question in several different ways. The participant felt the interviewers were not accepting her explanation of why she separated from a high paying position. She felt the interviewers interpreted her answer as dishonest. The finding of this survey revealed that participants responded adversely to interviewers perceived to be dishonest. In contrast, study participants responded positively to interviewers who were perceived as friendly, and honest.

Work hours and scheduling requirements of a position were commonly asked questions of interviewers by study participants. Several participants expressed concern about the impact of work requirements on family time. Participants who valued time spent with family members reviewed person-organization fit to ensure employment could be merged with the family structure with minimal interference.

The findings for the study revealed compensation as a factor that candidates considered when evaluating person-organization fit, although compensation did not rank as an emergent theme. Candidates who value material possessions or a certain lifestyle associate a higher pay with the ability to acquire these possessions or the lifestyle (Cable & Judge, 1997). These findings are important to the body of knowledge because employers must consider that candidates are determining 'fit' as the candidate moves through the employment recruitment process.

Methodological Implications

The groundwork of this study was phenomenological. Qualitative research can be conducted in four frameworks, case study, grounded theory, ethnography, and phenomenological (Christensen, et al., 2011). A phenomenological framework allowed the researcher to gain insight into the study participants' decision to continue or abort an employment recruitment process.

The researcher could have used grounded theory had there been more research in regards to candidates who sought employment and the factors that cause these graduates to abort or continue in the recruitment process. Once more research has been completed it would benefit other researchers to explore the grounded theory in order to develop a specific theoretical lens for the study topic.

Creswell (2007) stated that researchers who use a qualitative process seek to answer questions by collecting data through interviews and literature. This research employed both elements. The researcher utilized 5 open-ended interview questions with subsequent probing sub-questions as the data collection instrument. Employing a qualitative phenomenological approach provided the researcher a real-life, lived perspective into a candidates' decision to complete, abort or withdraw from the employment recruitment process.

Each participant's identity was concealed by the issuance of a numeric alpha system. Participants were coded P1, P2, P3, and so forth. This coding ensured participant's identity would remain confidential. This coding allowed ease in the identification of themes. Collecting qualitative data is distinct because of the collection of data regarding lived experiences and perceptions (Seidman, 1998). Each of the participant experiences aided in the identification of influences that impact an applicant's decision to abort or complete the employment recruitment process.

Practical Implications

The results of this study may influence the recruitment experience for candidates and those organizations wishing to employ them. Organizations are losing qualified candidates who apply for employment within the employment recruitment process (Dineen & Williamson, 2012). Results of this study supported this finding as all participants had aborted or withdrew from an employment recruitment process. The participants cited the interview experience as the factor in the employment recruitment process that facilitated how the participants' feelings changed as they progressed. The interview process is totally within the control of the employer to evaluate and make required changes to facilitate a participant's move forward.

The results of the study also revealed that those factors that adversely affected the experiences and perceptions of the participants were under the control of the employer. Participants were seeking information about job details. The interview was the number one reason listed by participants for aborting the employment recruitment process or continuing in the process. Each step in an organization's employment recruitment process must facilitate that each job applicant has a positive candidate experience (Ployhart, 2006).

There is an ongoing need for qualified employees within organizations (United States Bureau of Statistics, 2012). Occupations that require a college degree for entry are expected to grow faster than occupations that require a high school diploma or less (Slaughter & Greguras, 2009). Applicants are an ongoing source of qualified candidates. This study revealed that employers are losing these qualified candidates prior to the completion of the employment recruitment process. The loss of these qualified candidates will result in an employer's inability to fill the projected vacancies due to Baby Boomers exiting the workforce. Vacant positions will impact customer service company-wide, financial stability within the market, and industry competitiveness.

There is a scarceness of literature that recognizes and examines recruitment practices that consider candidates as a qualified pool of candidates and who have later lost those same candidates in the employment recruitment process. The incorporation of the results of this study provides a comprehensive document that offer factors in the employment recruitment process for recruiters in those organizations to review to increase the retention of candidates throughout the process. Although the employment recruitment process is not a new phenomenon, it is one that necessitates unending consideration and examination.

Limitations

Findings from this study should be considered in light of its limitations. The keyword analysis yielded 10 themes based on study participants' responses. The use of open-ended questions as the study instrument may have contributed to the lack of consistency among participants' responses. Another study using a different instrumentation may yield a more consistent participant response to questions.

The requirements were that participants had voluntarily disengaged or withdrew from one recruitment employment process and accepted an employment offer from another organization. This may have limited the research results by omitting candidates who participated in one of the employment recruitment processes. Information from either of these processes can yield information to assist employers.

Semi-structured open-ended questions were the instrument for data collection for the study. The length of time that was required for participation in the study due to the type of instrument used may have contributed to the decline of potential study participants. Fifteen candidates participated in the study. Using Nvivo10© software, theoretical analysis and keyword recognition saturation occurred at 15 participants. This total represented a sufficient quantity of participants for study saturation.

Recommendations

This study explored the lived experiences and perceptions of candidates who voluntarily disengaged or withdrew from one recruitment employment process and who accepted an employment offer from another organization. College and employer partnerships are an immediate source of qualified talent for hiring organizations.

166

These candidates are needed to replace the existing Baby Boomers in the work force who are expected to leave the labor market by year 2022. As these graduates enter the work force, they bring with them the recent knowledge of their field, and the most recent technological innovations of their industry. The following recommendations are based on the current study findings.

College Career Services Recommendations

The relationship between college career services and employers are that of a partnership. Employers desire to hire candidates. And colleges desire that the employment recruitment process results in the hiring of the student. The results of this study could be used by career services to develop training or workshops and a helpful checklist for employers who are recruiting college graduates.

The checklist may include the following areas of an employer's recruitment process for the employers to analyze. These include: position postings, application acknowledgement, timely notification of candidates move to next step in the process, and all aspects of the interview process. The interview process was cited as the reason for candidates continuing or withdrawing from the employment recruitment process.

Employers could analyze the type of interview selected, the number of interview questions, the quantity of interviewers, how interview questions are structured, and non- verbal behavior in interviews, and how to provide the most effective experience for the candidates.

Employer Recommendations

Employers need to be aware of the impact the entire recruiting experience or process has on a candidate who is a recent college graduate. Employers need to also acknowledge an employment application within a week. Participant responses strongly suggest that employers will benefit from acknowledging applicant interest in less than a week. While this study sought to understand several factors in the employment recruitment process, and its role in the applicant's decision-making to abort or continue, the question of application acknowledgement elicited several expressive feelings and emotions from candidates that should not go unaddressed. Employers can monitor, evaluate, and adjust the application acknowledgement process. This is within an organization's control to make the necessary adjustments. Investigating the application acknowledgement rate on a regular basis ensures that adjustments can be made to insure that candidates receive acknowledgements within a week of application. This analysis can be done by the creation of automated reports in the human resources application tracking system that compares the acknowledgement date against the application date. By employers identifying those factors that contribute to a delay in application acknowledgement, and adjusting these factors, candidates are informed that employment information has been received within a week.

The next recommendation is for employers to notify candidates of advancement to the next step in the employment recruitment process within a week of the employment interview. Participant responses revealed that employers are not notifying candidates of advancement in the recruitment process within a week of the interview. At least one applicant accepted another employment offer believing she was no longer being considered for a position. Favorable interaction of timely notification of movement to the next step within the employment recruitment process encourages applicant movement through the process that leads to offer acceptance by the candidate. The analysis of participants' responses suggested that potential employers will benefit from communicating with candidates at the earliest point the employer is aware of its interest in furthering the candidate in the employment recruitment process.

Another recommendation is for employers to routinely analyze each element of the interview process from questions asked, length of interview, maximum number of interviewers, and disposition of interviewers; to assess if each element of the employment process is portraying the intended image of the organization. The interview process was the common factor among participants who decided to continue or abort the employment recruitment process. Any undesirable encounter from employment application to the interview process may cause the applicant to seek employment elsewhere.

Participant responses suggest potential employers should strive to provide as many details about the vacant position as possible throughout the employment process. Another recommendation is for employers to incorporate additional job details within each step of the employment recruitment process. This can be done by publishing detailed position advertisements. Employer representatives may share the formal job description at the employment interview to be read by the candidate prior to conducting the interview. Interview questions are created from the tasks and responsibilities of the position along with realistic scenarios to demonstrate a true position description and work environment profile for the candidate to consider.

A final recommendation is for employers to solicit feedback from candidates who have experienced their employment recruitment process. This can be accomplished by administering a brief electronic questionnaire. This questionnaire would inquire about the ease of movement through the human resources application software program. Feedback regarding the interview process can be attained by the completion of the anonymous online survey using www.surveymonkey.com within thirty days of the interview. This survey would solicit feedback about the demeanor of interviewers, suitability of interview questions, and the duration of the entire interview process. Information from the applicant responses would be used to address those areas in the employment recruitment process that does not facilitate a candidates' move to the next step.

Recommendations for Further Research

Based on findings discussed in the previous chapter, opportunities for future research exist regarding the candidates who are seeking employment in any industry. Of the 201 email inquiries, only 15 participants provided (0.07%) consent to be interviewed as part of the study. Saturation of themes occurred at 15 participants. The study could have advanced from a bigger populace. Participants of this study were recent employment candidates. Future research is recommended to analyze the experiences of participants seeking their first professional employment since college, outside of the 12-month restriction used for this study. A study minus the 12-month limit may yield different results.

College recruiters representing hiring organizations and organizational leaders can benefit from the results of this study. College recruiters spend a significant amount of time traveling to college campuses to inform recent graduates about their organization's employment opportunities and benefits. The return on the recruiter's investment is a successful qualified hire from that college visit. Organizational leaders could review and analyze all elements of the employment recruitment process on a routine basis. Leaders could ensure all steps in the employment process facilitate an applicant move to the next step in the process. Recommendations for conducting future research should consist of the following:

1. Change the method from qualitative to mixed methods to allow for gathering the statistical data along with the descriptive information for a comparison of the study's findings.

2. Change the phenomenological study to a case study to gain an understanding of the candidates' perceptions post job offer acceptance and throughout the employment tenure.

3. Change the geographical location to gain a broader understanding of how candidates across a wider geographical spectrum perceive the phenomenon.

Summary

Chapter 5 included a discussion of the research questions, limitations, assumptions, findings and the identified themes, and recommendations for future research. The themes identified were based on a keyword analysis of study participants' responses. The results of this study will assist employers in retaining candidates throughout the employment recruitment process.

Study participants referenced the employment interview process as a factor in the participants' decision to continue or withdrew from the employment recruitment process. Participants cited the interview questions, the temperament of the interviewers, and the number of employer representatives conducting the interview as specific reasons for their decision to continue or disengage the employment recruitment process. As employers recruit, to hire employees to replace exiting Baby Boomers, employer representatives will need to retain the interest of candidates throughout the employment process to obtain success in filling vacated positions.

These results contribute to the body of knowledge of candidates' recruiting experiences. Employers can benefit from the study results and use the results to address those factors in the organization that do not contribute to employment candidates moving throughout the entire recruitment process. The study results revealed that employers could regularly evaluate and identify those elements in the employment recruitment process that do not facilitate a candidate's movement throughout the process.

References

Aiman-Smith, L., Bauer, T., & Cable, D. M. (2001). Are you attracted? Do you intend to pursue? A recruiting policy-capturing study. *Journal of Business and Psychology, 16*(2), 219-237. doi:10.1023/A:101157116322

Al-Hamadan, Z. (2010). Deciding on a mixed-methods design in a doctoral study. *Nurse Researcher*, 45-56. doi:10.7748/NR2010.10.18.1.45.C8047

Alwi, S. F. (2009). Online corporate brand images and consumer loyalty. *International Journal of Business and Society, 10*(2), 1-9.

Anaya, P. (2013). *How to solve a problem-Eight easy steps to find the solution.* Retrieved October 28, 2013, from Ezine Articles: http://ezinearticles.com/?How-to-Solve-a- Problem---Eight-Easy-Steps-to-Find-the-Solution

Armache, J. (2011). Understanding the various management philosophies. *Leadership & Organizational Management Journal, 2011*(1), 63-71.

Bak, O. (2011). The role of qualitative research in a mixed methods study. *Qualitative Research Journal, 11*(2), 76-84. doi:10.3316/QRJ1102076

Bateman, T. S., & Snell, S. A. (2009).*Management: Leading & collaborating in the competitive world* (8th ed.). Boston: McGraw-Hill Irwin.

Bermudez-Edo, M., Hurtado-Torres, N., & Aragon-Correa, J. A. (2010). The importance of trusting beliefs linked to the corporate website for diffusion of recruiting-related online innovations. *Information Technology Management, 11*, 177-189. Retrieved from http://dx.doi.org/10.1007/s10799-010-0074-1

Bernardian, H. J., Richey, B. E., & Castro, S. L. (2011). Mandatory and binding arbitration: Effects on employee attitudes and recruiting results. *Human Resource Management, 50*(2), 175-200. Retrieved from http://dx.doi.org/10.1002/hrm.20417

Bosak, J., & Sczesny, S. (2008). Am I the right candidate? Self-ascribed fit of women and men to a leadership position. *Sex Roles, 58*, 682-688. doi:10.1007/s11199- 007-9380-4

Boswell, W. R., Zimmerman, R. D., & Swider, B. W. (2011). Employee job search: Toward and understanding of search context and search objectives. *Journal of Management, 38*(1), 129-163. doi:10.1177/0149206311421829

Brainerd, C., & Reyna, V. (2002).Fuzzy-trace theory and false memory. *Department of Special Education, Rehabilitation, and School Psychology, and Department of Medicine, 11*(5).doi:10.1111/1467-8721.00192

Brown, H. (2011). The role of emotion in decision-making. *The Journal of Adult Protection, 13*(4), 194-202. Retrieved from http://dx.doi.org/10.1108/14668201111177932

Cable, D. M., & Graham, M. E. (2000).The determinants of job seekers' reputation perceptions. *Journal of Organizational Behavior, 21*, 929-947. doi:10.1002/1099-1379(200012)21:%::AID-JOB63%3E3.0.CO;2-0

Cable, D. M., & Judge, T. A. (1997). Pay preferences and job search decisions: A person- organization fit perspective. *Personnel Psychology*, 317-348.

Cable, D. M., & Kang, Y. T. (2006). Managing job seekers' organizational image beliefs: The role of media richness and media credibility. *Journal of Applied Psychology, 91*(4), 828-840. Retrieved fromhttp://dx.doi.org/10.1037/0021-9010.91.4.828

Cable, D., & Parson, C. K. (2001). Socialization tactics and person-organization fit. *Socialization tactics and person-organization fit, 54*(1), 1-23. Retrieved from http://dx.doi.org/10.1111/j.1744-6570.2001.tb00083.x

Caffarella, R. S., & Barnett, B. G. (2000).Teaching doctoral students to become scholarly writers: The importance of giving and receiving critiques. *Studies in Higher Education, 25*(1), 39-52. doi:10.1080/030750700116000

Campion, M., Palmer, D., & Campion, J. (1997).A review of structure in the selection interview. *Personnel Psychology, 50*, 655-702.

Carless, S., & Imber, A. (2007). The influence of perceived interviewer and job organizational characteristics on applicant attraction and job choice intentions: The role of applicant anxiety. *International Journal of Selection and Assessment, 15*(4), 359-371. Retrieved from http://dx.doi.org/10.1111/j.1468-2389.2007.00395.x

Caspar, R., & Peytcheva, E. (2011, November 4). Cross-Cultural Survey Guidelines. *Pretesting*, 1-31.

Chapman, D. S., & Webster, J. (2003, June/September). The use of technologies in the recruiting, screening, and selection processes for job candidates. *International Journal of Selection and Assessment, 11*(2/3), 113-120. doi:10.1111/1468- 2389.00234

Christensen, L. B., Johnson, R. B., & Turner, L. A. (2011).*Research Methods, Design, and Analysis.* Allyn & Bacon.

Coldwell, D. A., Meurs, N. v., & Marsh, P. J. (2008). The effects of person-organization ethical fit on employee attraction and retention: Towards a testable explanatory model. *Journal of Business Ethics*, 611-622. doi:10.1007/s10551-007-9371-y

Cole, M., & Avison, D. (2007).The potential of hermeneutics in information systems research. *European Journal of Information Systems, 16*, 820-833. Retrieved from http://dx.doi.org/10.1057/palgrave.ejis.3000725

Collins, C. J., & Kanar, A. M. (2013).Employer brand equity and recruitment research.In A. Kanar, *Oxford handbook of recruitment* (pp. 284-297). Retrieved from http://dx.doi.org/10.1093/oxfordhb/9780199756094.013.0016

Collins, C. J., & Stevens, C. (2002). The relationship between early recruitment related activities and the application decisions of new labor market entrants: A brand equity approach to recruitment. *Journal of Applied Psychology, 87*, 1121-1133. Retrieved from http://dx.doi.org/10.1037/0021-9010.87.6.1121

Converse, M. (2012). Philosophy of phenomenology: How understanding aids research.

Nurse Researcher, 20(1), 28-32. Retrieved from http://dx.doi.org/10.7748/nr2012.09.20.1.28.c9305

Cooman, R. A., & Pepermans, R. (2012).Portraying fitting values in job advertisements. *Personnel Review, 41*(2), 216-232. doi:10.1108/0048348121200042

Creswell, J. W. (2007). *Qualitative inquiry & research design: Choosing among five approaches* (2nd ed.). Thousand Oaks, CA: Sage.

Crist, J. D., & Tanner, C. A. (2003).Interpretation/analysis methods in hermeneutic interpretive phenomenology. *Nursing Research, 52*(3), 202-205.doi:10.1097/00006199-200305000-00011

Davidson, B. (2000, December 15). *Hiring an employee how much does it cost?* Retrieved from Workforce: http://www.workforce.com/articles/hiring-an- employee-how-much-does-it-cost

Davies, G., & Chun, R. (2012). Employee as symbol: Stereotypical age effects on corporate brand associations. *European Journal of Marketing, 46*(5), 663-683. Retrieved from http://dx.doi.org/10.1108/03090561211212467

DeGroot, T., & Gooty, J. (2009). Can nonverbal cues be used to make meaningful personality attributions in employment interviews? *Journal of Business and Psychology, 24*(2), 179-192. Retrieved from http://dx.doi.org/10.1007/s10869-009-9098-0

Denzin, N., & Lincoln, Y. (2003).*The landscape of qualitative research: Theories and issues* (2nd ed.). London: Sage Publications.

Dineen, B. R., & Williamson, I. O. (2012). Screening-oriented recruitment messages: Antecedents and relationships with applicant pool quality. *Human Resource Management, 51*(3), 343-360. doi:10.1002/hrm.21476

(2013). *Employment Projections 2012-2022.* Washington D. C.: Bureau of Labor Statistics: U.S. Department of Labor.

Feldman, D. C., Bearden, W. O., & Hardesty, D. M. (2006).Varying the content of job advertisements. *Journal of Advertising, 35*(1), 123-141. Retrieved from http://dx.doi.org/10.2753/JOA0091-3367350108

Fishbein, M., & Ajzen, I. (1975).*Belief, attitude, intention and behavior: An introduction to theory and research.* Reading, MA: Addison-Wesley.

Gatewood, R. D., Gowan, M. A., & Lautenschlager, G. J. (1993).Corporate image, recruitment image, and initial job choice decisions. *Academy of Management Journal, 36*(2), 414-427. doi:10.2307/256530

Gibbs, G. R. (2013). Using CAQDAS programs. In *Handbook of qualitative data analysis.* London: Sage.

Goldberg, C. B., & Allen, D. G. (2008). Black and white and read all over: Race differences in reactions to recruitment websites. *Human Resource Management, 47*(2), 217-236. doi:10.1002/hrm.20209

Gomes, D. R., & Neves, J. (2010). Employer branding constrains candidates' job seeking behavior. *Revista de Psicologfa y de las Organizations, 26*(3), 223-234. Retrieved from http://dx.doi.org/10.5093/tr2010v26n3a6

Gomes, D., & Neves, J. (2011).Organizational attractiveness and prospective candidates' intentions to apply. *Personnel Review, 40*(6), 684-699. doi:10.1108/00483481111169634

Griffiths, F. (1996). Qualitative research: The Research Questions it can help answer, the methods it uses, the assumptions behind the research questions and what influences the direction of research. A summary of the panel discussion at the conference 'Exploring qualitative. *Family Practice, 13*(1). Retrieved from http://dx.doi.org/10.1093/oxfordjournals.fampra.a018281

Hemphill, E., & Kulik, C. T. (2011).Segmenting a general practitioner market to improve recruitment outcomes. *Australian Health Review, 35*, 117-123. doi:10.1071/AH09802

Hicks, T. (1999, April).*Seven steps for effective problem solving in the workplace.* Retrieved October 28, 2013, from Mediate.com: http://mediate.com/pfriendly.cfm?id=170

Huffcutt, A. I., Van Iddekinge, C., & Roth, P. L. (2011). Understanding applicant behavior in employment interviews: A theoretical model of interviewee performance. *Human Resource Management Review, 21*, 353-367. doi:10.1016/j.hrmr.2011.05.03

Hughes, R. L., Ginnett, R. C., & Curphy, G. J. (1995).Understanding and influencing follower motivation. In W. J. Thomas, *The leader's companion: Insights on leadership through the ages* (pp. 327-338). New York: The Free Press.

Hurst, J. L., & Good, L. K. (2009). Generation Y and career choice: The impact of retail career perceptions, expectations and entitlement perceptions. *Career Development International, 14*(6), 570-593. doi:10.1108/13620430910997303

Judge, Bretz, & T.A.R.D. (1992).Effects of work values on job choice decisions. *Journal of Applied Psychology, 77*, 261-271. Retrieved from http://dx.doi.org/10.1037/0021-9010.77.3.261

Kartha, D. (2012, March 2). *6 Steps to decision-making process.* Retrieved October 10, 2013, from Buzzle: http://www.buzzle.com/articles/6-steps-to-decision-making-process.html

Kim, T.-Y., Cable, D. M., & Kim, S.-P. (2005). Socialization tactics, employee proactivity, and person-organization fit. *Journal of Applied Psychology, 90*(2), 232-241. Retrieved from http://dx.doi.org/10.1037/0021-9010.90.2.232

Kulkarni, M., & Nithyanand, S. (2013).Social influence and job choice decisions. *Employee Relations, 35*(2), 139-156. doi:10.1108/01425451311287844

Kvale, S. (1996).*An introduction to qualitative research interviewing.* Thousand Oaks: Sage Publications.

Leedy, P., & Ormrod, J. E. (2010).*Practical research: Planning and design* (9th ed.). Merrill.

Lehmann, I., & Konstam, V. (2011).Growing up perfect: Perfectionism, problematic internet use, and career indecision in emerging adults. *Journal of Counseling & Development, 89*, 155-162. doi:10.1002/j.1556-6678.2011.tb00073.x

Lievens, F., Hoye, G. V., & Schreurs, B. (2005).Examining the relationship between employer knowledge dimensions and organizational attractiveness: An application in a military context. *Journal of Occupational and Organizational Psychology, 78*(4), 553-

181

572. doi:10.1348/09631790x26688

Lincoln, Y., & Guba, E. (1985).*Naturalistic inquiry*. Newbury Park: Sage Publications.

Lowhorn, G. L. (2003). *Qualitative and quantitative research: How to choose the best design*. Virginia Beach: Regent University.

Lyons, B. D., & Marler, J. H. (2011). Got image? Examining organizational image in web recruitment. *Journal of Managerial Psychology, 26*(1), 58-76. doi:10.1108/02683941111099628

Ma, R., & Allen, D. G. (2009).Recruiting across cultures: A value-based model of recruitment. *Human Resource Management Review, 19*, 334-346. doi:10.1016/j.hrmr.2009.03.001

Macan, T. (2009). The employment interview: A review of current studies and directions for future research. *Human Resource Management Review, 19*, 203-218. doi:10.1016/j.hrmr.2009.03.006

Martin, C., Anderson, L., Cronin, B., Heinen, B., &Swetharanyan, S. (2010). Predicting job decisions in tomorrow's workforce. *Journal of Employment Counseling, 47*(4), 167-179. doi:10.1002/j.2161-1920.2010.tb00101.x

Martin, L. A. (2000). Effective data collection. *Total Quality Management, 11*(3), 341-344. Retrieved from http://dx.doi.org/10.1080/0954412006856

Maslow, A. (1943). A theory of human motivation. *Psychological Review, 50*(4), 370-396. Retrieved from http://dx.doi.org/10.1037/h0054346

McCarthy, J., Iddekinge, C., & Campion, M. (2010, Summer). Are highly structured job interviews resistant to demographic similarity effects? *Personnel Psychology, 63*(2), 325-359.

Mitchell, M. (2011).A reflection on the emotional potential of qualitative interviewing. *British Journal of Midwifery*, 653-656. Retrieved from http://dx.doi.org/10.12968/bjom.2011.19.10.653

Moustakas, C. (1994). *Phenomenological research methods.* Thousand Oaks, CA: Sage.

Neumann, W. L. (2006). *Social research methods: Qualitative and quantitative approaches.* Allyn and Bacon.

Nolan, K. P., & Harold, C. M. (2010). Fit with what? The influence of multiple self- concept images on organizational attraction. *The Journal of Occupational and Organizational Psychology, 83*(3), 645-662. doi:10.1348/096317909X465452

NVivo10©. (2013). Retrieved from QSR international: http://www.qsrinternational.com/products_nvivo.apx

Patton, M. Q. (2002). *Qualitative research and evaluation methods* (3rd ed.). Thousand Oaks, CA: Sage.

Ployhart, R. (2006). Staffing in the 21st century: New challenges and strategic opportunities. *Journal of Management, 32*, 868-897. Retrieved from http://dx.doi.org/10.1177/0149206306293625

Professional Employees. (2014, September 29). Retrieved from Department of Labor: http://www.dol.gov/whd/regs/compliance/fairpay/regulations_final.ht m

Rai, H., & Kothari, J. (2008). Recruitment advertising and corporate image: Interface between marketing and human resources. *South Asian Journal of Management, 15*(2), 47-60.

Ramaswami, A., & Dreher, G. F. (2010). Dynamics of mentoring relationships in India: A qualitative, exploratory study. *Human Resource Management, 49*(3), 501-530. doi:10.1002/hrm.20363

Reyan, V. F. (2004). How people make decisions that involve risk: A dual-processes approach. *Current Directions in Psychological Science, 13*(2), 60-66. doi:10.1111/j.0963-7214.2004.00275.x

Rhynes, S. L. (1991). Recruitment, job choice, and post-hire consequences: A call for new research directions. In M. D. Dubbette, & L. M. Hough, *Handbook of Industrial and Organizational Psychology* (2nd ed., pp. 399-444). Palo Alto, CA: Consulting Psychologists Press.

Richens, Y., & Smith, D. (2011).Applied qualitative research in maternity care: a reflection of the barriers to data collection with 'at-risk' populations. *Diversity in Health and Care*, 29-36.

Rubin, H., & Rubin, I. (2005).*Qualitative interviewing: The art of hearing data.* Thousand Oaks: Sage Publications.

Ryan, M. C., & Cronin, P. (2007).Step-by-step guide to critiquing research. Part 2: Qualitative research. *British Journal of Nursing*, 738-743.

Saks, A. M., & Uggerslev, K. L. (2010).Sequential and combined effects of recruitment information on applicant reactions. *Journal of Business Psychology, 25*(3), 351- 365.doi:10.1007/s10869-009-9142-0

Salkind, N. (2003). *Exploring research: The role and importance of research* (7th ed.).

Lawrence: Pearson Prentice Hall. Schreurs, B., Druart, C., Proost, K., & De Witte, K. (2009). Symbolic attributes and organizational attractiveness: The moderating effects of applicant personality. *International Journal of Selection and Assessment, 17*(1), 35-46. Retrieved from http://dx.doi.org/10.1111/j.1468-2389.2009.00449.x

Seidman, I. (1998). *Interviewing as qualitative research: A guide for researchers in education and the social sciences* (2nd ed.). New York, NY: Teachers College Press.

Simon, M. K. (2006). *Dissertation & scholarly research: A practical guide to start & complete your dissertation, thesis, or formal research project.* Dubuque, IA: Kendall/Hunt Publishing Company.

Slaughter, J. E., & Greguras, G. J. (2009). Initial attraction to organizations: The influence of trait inferences. *International Journal of Selection and Assessment, 17*(1), 1-18. doi:10.1111/j.1468-2389.2009.00447.x

Smith, A. D., & Rupp, W. (2004). Managerial challenges of e-recruiting. *Online Information Review, 28*(1), 61-74. doi:10.1108/14684520410522466 *Education,* 271-288. Retrieved from http://dx.doi.org/10.1080/03634520500442145

Strand, R., Levine, R., & Montgomery, D. (1981). Organizational entry preferences based upon social and personnel policies: An information integration perspective. *Organizational Behavior and Human Performance, 27*(1), 50-68. doi:10.1016/0030-5073(81)90038-6

Suptan, N. (2011). A role of socialization tactics on the perceived person-job fit of all new employers. *Proceedings of the European Conference on Management, Leadership & Governance* (pp. 394-401). Academic Conferences, Ltd.

Top 50 Major Employers in Hampton Roads. (2013, January 31). Retrieved April 22, 2013, from Pilot Online: http://media.hamptonroads.com/media/thevirginianpilot/pdf/advertising/Top50Ma jorEmployers.pdf

Trueman, M. (2012). Building brand value online: Exploring relationships between company and city brands. *European Journal of Marketing, 46*(7/8), 1013-1031. Retrieved from http://dx.doi.org/10.1108/03090561211230179

Tsai, W.-C., & Yang, I. W.-F. (2010). Does image matter to different job candidates: The influence of corporate image and applicant individual differences on organizational attractiveness. *International Journal of Selection and Assessment, 18*(1), 48-63. Retrieved from http://dx.doi.org/10.1111/j.1468-2389.2010.00488.x

Uggerslev, K., Fassina, N., & Kraichy, D. (2012).Recruiting through the stages: A meta- analytic test of predictors of applicant attraction at different stages of the recruiting process. *Personnel Psychology, 65*(3).doi:10.1111/j.1744- 6570.2012.01254.x

United States Bureau of Statistics. (2012, March). Retrieved from Employment trend costs: http://www.bls.gov/ncs/ect/ Vallaster, C., & Lindgreen, A. (2011). Corporate brand strategy formation: Brand actors and the situational context for a business-to-business brand. *Industrial Marketing Management, 40,* 1133-1143. Retrieved from http://dx.doi.org/10.1016/j.indmarman.2011.09.008

Vandermause, R. K. (2012). Being wholesome: The paradox of methamphetamine addiction and recovery-A hermeneutical phenomenological interpretation within an interdisciplinary, transmethodological study. *Qualitative Social Work, 11*(3), 299- 318. Retrieved from http://dx.doi.org/10.1177/1473325011401470

Walker, H. J., Berneth, J. B., Field, H. S., & Becton, J. B. (2012). Diversity cues on recruitment websites: Investigating the effects on job seekers' information processing. *Journal of Applied Psychology, 97*(1), 214-224. doi:10.1037/a0025847

Walker, S. (2011). The interview process and beyond. *The Bottom Line Managing Library, 24*(1), 41- 45.doi:10.1108/08880451111142042

Walter, B. v., Wentsel, D., & Tomczak, T. (2012).The effect of applicant-employee fit and temporal construal on employer attraction and pursuit intentions. *Journal of Occupational and Organizational Psychology*, 116-135. Retrieved from http://dx.doi.org/10.1348/2044-8325.002006 Watson, C. (2007).'Small stories' and the doing of professional identities in learning to teach. *Narrative Inquiry, 17*(2), 371-389.

Wayne, J. H., & Casper, W. J. (2012). Why does firm reputation in human resources policies influence college students? The mechanisms underlying job pursuit intentions. *Human Resource Management, 51*(1), 121-142. doi:10.1002.hrm.21461

Yue, V. Y. (2012). 'Role' and position': Job expectations and practices. *Asian Social Science, 8*(1), 12-16

Appendix: A: Interview Questions and Probes

1. Describe the employment application process that you experienced.

   a. If online, what feedback do you have about the online application system?

   b. How long did it take to receive acknowledgment of your application from the potential employer?

   c. Was this period acceptable to you?

   d. What form of feedback did you receive: written, phone call, or other?

   e. How did you feel about this method?

   f. What was the length of time from application acknowledgement to the next step in the employment recruitment process?

   g. How did you feel about this duration?

2. Describe your perceptions of the interview process from which you withdrew from consideration for employment?

   a. How did your feelings change or evolve as you

progressed through the interview?

How did the interviewers make you feel?

b. What information were you seeking in the employment interview from which you withdrew?

c. At what point in the interview process did you make the decision to withdraw?

3. Explain your perception of what could have prevented your withdrawal from the employment recruitment process?

4. Describe your perceptions of the interview process from which you accepted an offer of employment?

a. How did your feelings change or evolve as you progressed through the interview?

b. How did the interviewers make you feel?

5. What information were you were seeking in the employment interview from which you accepted an offer of employment? Explain your perception of why you continued in the employment recruitment process for the employer to whom you accepted a job offer?

6. Probes used in the interview will include the following:

   – Like

   – Explain

   – Tell me more about that

   – What did you mean when you said

   – Can you explain that further

www.ingramcontent.com/pod-product-compliance
Lightning Source LLC
Chambersburg PA
CBHW070714220326
41598CB00024BA/3142